Yak Y

Yak Yak Yak!

Mike Yaconelli's GUIDE TO Jerk-Free Christianity

Edited by James Tweed

Marshall Pickering
An Imprint of HarperCollinsPublishers

First published in Great Britain in 1991 by Marshall Pickering

Marshall Pickering is an imprint of
HarperCollinsReligious,
part of HarperCollins*Publishers*,
77–85 Fulham Palace Road
Hammersmith, London W6 8JB

Printed and bound in Great Britain by
HarperCollinsManufacturing, Glasgow

A catalogue record for this book
is available from the British Library

Contents

Editor's Preface

Mike Yaconelli has to be taken seriously, especially because of his wicked sense of humour and his eye for life's idiosyncrasies and absurdities. He lives in California (where else?), pastors a church for "people who don't like going to church" (his description) and edits what is probably the greatest – the only? – Christian satirical bi-monthly magazine in the world, *The Wittenburg Door*, now known simply as *The Door* – presumably because the folks in Wittenburg wanted their name back . . .

Mike is funny, especially when he's being deadly serious. And that's because he cares about the planet he lives on, the people he shares it with and also about his Christian faith and what it means. He's unpredictable, unflappable and unpronounceable (well, two out of three are true. Guess which ones). In an exclusive interview with *Strait* magazine in 1989 he cited evidence of the Holy Spirit's living in the heart of believers as being revealed by original thought plus "a mischievous look in the eye".

"The truth of the Gospel is that Christ makes our life 'more abundant'. Unfortunately we spiritualize it so it loses any practical understanding."

There ought to be a twinkle in a Christian's eye, he says. "Christians think fresh. We just don't think like other people do, we're able to think in new categories.

The trouble is that the Church has traded one form of cultural slavery for another. It has said, 'I'm not going to become programmed like our culture and I'm going to think Christianly', which usually means 'Now I'm going to think like Christians think'.

"What worries me is that the Church just seems to be rearranging the furniture, that Christians keep taking the same old truths and coming up with a new arrangement of them instead of coming up with new ways of living life, ways that change our ability to cope with paganism and secularism."

Yaconelli once saw a Peanuts cartoon that had particular resonance to him. Set on a huge ocean-going cruise liner, a character expounds some home-spun philosophy, remarking how "life is like a cruise ship – some people like to put their deck-chair at the ship's bows to see where they are going, other people like to put theirs at the stern to see where they have been." Charlie Brown then says, "Well, I can never get my deck-chair unfolded."

Neither can Mike. He says he's like Charlie Brown, asking on behalf of himself and all those like him, "How do you unfold this deck-chair anyway?"

So draw up your deck-chair. Sit down and enjoy the wit, wisdom and insight of one of the only theologians I know who makes you laugh until it hurts. If you feel your life is all messed up, this book is for you; if you don't, then you're probably not being honest.

Enjoy!

James Tweed
Assistant editor, *Strait*

1

Born Old

I love England, though to a Southern Californian like me, it always seems to be raining. Where I live we don't get much rain or snow, but when my first son was three years old I took him to see what snow was like. We travelled to Lake Arrowhead, and, typically, before we arrived all the snow had melted except for a 300-foot-long strip.

Actually it was fantastic, because when you have a three-year-old kid in tow they can't do much on their own. So I set him atop this 300-foot piece of ice on the sled we'd brought, let him go and watched him fly straight down that 300 feet of ice. At the bottom fifty feet of weeds, earth and leaves would stop him, but if that didn't there were a bunch of trees that did.

He kept on going down this thing and had a ball all day long. I'd go to the bottom, pull the sled up again and put him back on. Then, I made a tragic mistake. By 3 o'clock the snow started to melt and he was getting tired, so I said to my son, "OK, one more time".

Big mistake. Now, I don't know what goes through a three-year-old's mind, but my kid was up on that sled – he'd been going down straight every single time exactly the same way – and half-way down he turned around, gave me a weird look and pushed forward. He made a 90-degree turn – which was great, except there was only five feet of snow, then five feet of earth, followed by a ten-foot drop onto the road.

I wasn't prepared for that. One second I was just watching him; the next he flew off the snow, off the earth and right over the road. It was like a living "Roadrunner" cartoon, where characters run off cliffs and are suspended in mid-air. There was my little three-year-old boy on top of that sled, suspended over the road, giving me an "Uh, dad . . ." look. Then he dropped out of sight with a most horrible crash. I ran as fast as I could to get over there. The sled was upside down and my son lay on the ground. He looked at me, I stared at him. He said: "Did you see *that*?"

Well, after I'd changed my pants, I told him: "Don't do that to me", but the fact is when your kids grow up you have to let them go, and let them take little risks. You hope they'll not be that wild and crazy, but you do have to let them go and run with it. And if we're going to be Christians in the nineties we'll have to start taking risks and become known for stepping out and going beyond where ordinary people are.

Christians are very different people. We're not predictable. It makes me so angry how we always want Christians to say the same things and act in the same way. The beauty of the 1990s is that I think we're breaking free of that a little bit. Christians can now allow Jesus, as he speaks in their lives, to go a completely different way than somebody else does.

I started a church a number of years ago and we've had some strange folks show up. One Sunday morning a girl, who was a leftover from the sixties, came to the service. Her hair was super-kinky and super-long, and went straight out like one of those things that spins around in a car wash. Everybody was freaked out by her. The church people went: "Uh oh, who is she?" They didn't even know her, but their non-Christian radar was going crazy. She came in, sat down and attended our church for two years without ever saying a word.

One Sunday morning, right in the middle of my sermon, she stood up and said: "Could I say something?" What are you going to do? You're not going to say: "No. Sit down." Of course I let her, but like the rest of the congregation I was totally freaked out, and I thought: "Here we go, she's going to talk about health food." I had no idea what was going to happen. Everybody hushed and she said: "I've been coming to this church for two years and I've been watching you people and looking at what the Christian faith is about. I have to tell you that sometime during this week it finally all gelled for me and Christ became a real part of my life. I became a Christian." All the old people were muttering: "Oh Lord . . . when is she going to get a haircut . . ."

Unfortunately she didn't stop there. "In fact, I've really understood what it's like to know Christ because I've had an unbelievably s – – – – y week." (It wasn't until after the service that I told this girl not to use the word "week" in a testimony . . .) People got very upset because she used a swear word and they never heard anything else. Now I'm not suggesting we all use bar-room language in our conversations and testimonies, but at that particular moment it didn't really matter. What she was doing was sharing what Jesus meant in her life the only way she knew how. And we all imposed our own standards of religious-speak on her. We should have just listened to what she had to say and enjoyed it, for it would have been so refreshing, unique and great. But we couldn't do that.

To try and explain what it means to be a Christian in the 1990s there are a number of characteristics to consider.

The first is, that we have a real sense of confidence in God's love. I am convinced one of the biggest problems we have today is that people are basically afraid of God. Many of us many deny this: "Not me, I'm not afraid of God." But I don't mean walking around and cowering every five minutes. When I was younger I remember going to my church Youth Group, and afterwards I'd snog my brains out with my girlfriend. Next morning I'd wake up and know God was going to dissolve my lips . . .

That was the kind of fear I had of God. I knew he was going around saying: "Don't, don't, don't do that . . . that's it, goodbye!!" That's really what I'm talking about. It's the kind of attitude that says: "I can sort of serve God, I can sort of believe in God, but I'm not really going to give God all of my life for, if I do, he's going to ruin it. He's going to figure out what I like to do and tell me I can't do it. He's going to find the one place I don't want to go and that's where he's going to send me." There's a deep sense in all of our hearts of, "I'm so afraid, I don't really trust God", that if I give God my whole life he's going to ruin it.

When I talk to teenagers about sex, I often say I'm going to talk about it and then I don't (that keeps them there right to the end of the meeting). People have a weird notion about God, that he made sex by accident, and that he didn't make sex to be enjoyable. Of course

God made it! He knows exactly what it's about, he's not embarrassed or ashamed about it, but he made it to be contained in the commitment of marriage. And he's not apologetic about it.

I get the feeling some people don't believe that; like God made sex and then frowned: "Ooh! Whoops! Now I'm going to have to make a law against it . . ." God made it. He understands it, and the fact that you and I must learn to say no and wait until we're married is not something God is doing to punish us. He's doing it to salvage sex, to save it and to make it what it ought to be.

God has created us in such a way that he *wants* us to enjoy life and wants us to know what it's all about. But I'm convinced that people today are afraid of giving their whole hearts and lives to God.

When I play hide-and-seek with my kids I add a new dimension called "total fear". Once, when my boys were three and five years old, they had the audacity to try and find me, so when they did I'd make them pay by scaring the life out of them. My kids knew those were the rules. One night I hid in my bedroom. My two little boys were in the kitchen holding hands, totally freaked out already, they just kept counting – they went to about a thousand – and didn't want to stop. They stood there and the elder whispered: "He's in the cupboard", and the younger boy replied: "You look", and they had a big argument.

Finally they both walked over to the cupboard and opened the door. Of course I wasn't in there. Then I did what every parent does when they do that: I yelled: "Hey!" The elder deduced: "He's not in the cupboard." They walked down the hallway, waiting to go in –

all they'd got to do was turn on the light, it was no big deal, but they didn't do it. I was behind the door. They both came in real slowly, and as soon as I saw the elder boy's head I leapt out and screamed: "AAAAAGGGHHHH!!!" They ran all over the place, bumping into and tripping over each other, until, finally, they looked at me then back at each other, and said: "What are we *doing*? This is our dad. We don't have to be afraid – ATTACK!!" And they did.

We don't need to be afraid of God. What are we doing? He's our papa, our daddy, our abba. We can attack! We can interrupt him and butt in whenever we want to. I don't know what it is with people about God. They get this mystical, weird, unbelievable thing so that when they pray they change their whole personality. They're super-bubbly and normal until someone asks: "Mike, would you like to pray?" "OK, sure," then their voice becomes a drone, "Out of the mountain . . ."

Haven't you ever got angry with God and just wanted to tell him so, with gritted teeth: "GOD, I'M SO ANGRY!!!" And God goes: "Oh yeah?", turns over and goes back to sleep. God's *not* going to do that. We can be open with God, and share what we really feel, because he is our papa, our daddy – that's what "abba" means – and that's the kind of God we serve. I wish we could all get over our fear of God and learn how to love him, give ourselves to him and realize he's not out to get us or ruin our lives. Rather, he's out to give us life – that's what our whole faith in God is.

The second thing to realize, especially these days with the conservative Church growing like it is, is how Christians are sometimes cocky and arrogant. That has always bothered me, and I think it also bothers people who aren't Christians. It's like: "I used to be a slob and a slut like you, but now I've found Jesus I'm totally cool, and if you don't want to continue to be a scumbag you can respond to that Christ just like I did." It's almost that attitude. We act like we're *almost* better, as though we want people who aren't Christians to find out how bad it is. We want to prove to them what an abundant life we have by pointing out the rotten life they have.

People sense that arrogance and cockiness in Christians. Surely, of all people to be arrogant and cocky, it shouldn't be us. We know *exactly* what kind of people we are, and we know exactly what kind of people they are because we know ourselves. There're no illusions. When I walk into church on Sunday morning I'm unshockable, but everybody ought to be shocked that I'm there. When I walk in they ought to be saying: "Yaconelli, what are *you* doing here? This is church. This is for religious people, for good people." I know, though that's untrue — it's a place for people who are sick and for those who know what's wrong with them. That's why I'm here. And that's why all of us are there. No one is surprised. So when anybody walks in we're glad to see them, for we recognize they're just like us.

John Duckworth has written a great book called *The Man Who Built His House Upon The Rock*. It is an incredible rendition of the parable Jesus told about the man who built his house upon the sand and the other who built his house upon the rock:

Behold, there was a man who built his house upon the rock. When he had finished building his house upon a rock he laughs saying: "Oh, how wise I am to build my house upon a rock and how foolish is the man next door who built his house upon the sand, for it is written that when the rain descends and the floods come and the winds blow and beat upon these houses, the one founded upon the rock will fall not, but great will be the fall of the house built upon the sand. Ha, ha, ha, ha."

So, laughing, the man who built his house upon a rock went into his house and locked the door. "Now, I'm going to relax and wait for the storm warnings," he said, "for my house is founded safe upon a rock."

He did wait, and he waited . . . and he waited. Nothing happened. There was no rain, no flood, no wind – not even a mild drizzle. "Hey! Wait a minute!" said the man who built his house upon a rock, "There's supposed to be a big storm and the house built upon the sand is supposed to fall down. Everybody knows that!"

So he watched the sky, hoping for a hurricane or at least a major hailstorm. But there was nothing. "Well," the man said, perplexed, "I'm sure that storm will come along any minute now. In the meantime, that man who built his house upon the sand must be *pretty* nervous. I'll bet he's having a terrible time in that flimsy little house of his."

Chuckling smugly, he looked over at the house upon the sand. He expected to see his neighbour pacing anxiously back and forth, worried about a storm. But the neighbour was smiling and laughing, making sandcastles with his friends outside the house. They all seemed to be having a great time. "This is outrageous!", said the man who built his house on the rock. "These people should be miserable, not happy.

They should be begging for shelter in my house, hoping to escape the rain and the floods and the wind."

He continued to listen to the weather reports, waiting for the storm to arrive, but the skies remained clear. One day, however, the man heard noises from next door. They were the noises of pounding and yelling. "Aha!" he said. "At last the storm has come and my neighbour's house upon the sand is falling. How great will be the fall of it!" But when he rushed to the window he discovered his neighbour was turning the house upon the sand into a luxury beach-front resort. The neighbour was grinning from ear to ear, wearing an expensive suit, studying blueprints and directing work crews. Soon a fancy car drew up and a beautiful woman dressed in a mink coat got out and gave him a kiss.

"Where's the storm?" bellowed the man who built his house upon the rock. "The wise man builds his house upon the rock, the foolish man builds his house upon the sand, and the rains come tumbling down. Everybody knows that!"

Behold, the rains did come tumbling down, but they tumbled only on the house that had been built upon the rock. Not a drop fell upon the house that had been built upon the sand. "Why me?" moaned the man who had built his house upon a rock, "My house may stand firm, but I have to patch the rough, clean the gutters, bail out the basement. What does my neighbour do? Nothing."

So it was that in the months and years that followed, the man who built his house upon the sand got richer and richer, more and more successful, happier and happier. The man who built his house upon the rock patched the rough, cleaned the gutters and bailed out the basement.

Finally, years and years after he had built his house upon the rock, the man threw up his hands. "I give up!" he said. "I've waited and waited, watched the sky, patched and cleaned and bailed. A record rainfall's descended on *my* house and there's never so much as a mist on my neighbour's. Any fool can see there's not going to be a storm."

With that he packed his suitcase and went next door to the luxury beach-front resort built upon the sand. "If you can't beat 'em, join 'em", he said.

That very night, of course, the rain descended, and the floods came and the winds blew and beat upon both those houses. The one that was built upon the sand fell, and great was the fall of it. The other one fell not, for it was founded upon a rock. Too bad nobody was home.

*   *   *

That kind of cockiness and arrogance in the Church is picked up by our culture. We have nothing to be cocky or arrogant about. We are so graced of God just to be his family that it's almost embarrassing. We ought to be embarrassed rather than cocky. We ought to be humbled by the incredible gracious and kind love of our Father.

The third characteristic, and this may seem weird in this day and age, is tenderness. I think it is needed more than anything else today. I don't see many *tender* people any more. This is the macho age. Men don't have to be tender, but strong. But as I talk to women I've noticed they're asking for tenderness in men, that they're kind and have a very softness about them. And that's what this culture is looking for – Christians who are kind and tender.

Remember the woman caught in adultery? I read it all the time. I don't have to read it, I see it happening all the time. But remember how the Pharisees decided they were going to really get Jesus with this one and so they caught a woman *right in the act* of adultery. I've always wondered how those guys knew where she lived . . . They brought her to Jesus, probably partially clothed – a totally humiliating experience – in front of thousands of people right there in the Temple. Jesus stood there and here's this women, totally humiliated, with everybody looking and yelling at her, making fun of her and degrading her – all the horrible things that people tend to do when they find somebody like that.

Jesus then got down on his hands and knees and began to draw in the sand. You know why he did that? Because we need a reason for theological colleges. Somebody's got to spend their time wondering, "I wonder what he was writing down there? What do you think, Bob?" Think about it for a moment yourself. Here's this crowd. They're all looking at the woman, all their attention is on her, and Jesus, *without saying a single word*, causes the entire crowd to take their gaze off her and move it on to him. Talk about tenderness! He didn't say a word. Everybody in that crowd was just like us – "What's he doing? What's he writing? Get out of my way!" All their attention switches from the woman to Jesus. That's tenderness.

Not enough of us are tender and soft, saying thank you, telling people we love them, giving them little notes here and there to affirm them. When did you last receive a note from someone close to you that said you're really a good person? A lot of us have received messages saying we're jerks, but that's not what I mean. Just a note saying: "You are really special." So many of us wouldn't know what to do if we received one. If somebody close to us told us what a good person we are we'd probably be brought up short, murmur: "Gosh, gee", then go to our folks and say: "See? I'm not so bad after all!" That kind of tenderness is lost and I think it's time we began to find it.

The next characteristic, compassion, is similar. One way we develop compassion is not by talking about it but by going to where there's a need, seeing the need and being overwhelmed by it. We want to sit around and have our compassion be something that's emotional and sentimental, but we won't allow that compassion to alter how we live. We need to put ourselves in a place where people in need are all around us, so that we begin to smell, feel and develop a real burden for those people.

One of the reasons we don't have very many people go on the mission field any more is that we're all compassionate from a distance. I can send £10 and support a kid in Africa, but I don't have to go. It's great that we support people with our money but it's even better if we go with our bodies and spend some time there. Once there we'll sense that compassion and it'll change the way we live and how we spend our money.

The next characteristic is uniqueness. The Bible says we're all parts of the Body of Christ. Some of us are arms, others legs, some are rear ends – I know who they are – but each of us has a different function in the Body, and we ought to be proud and excited about it.

Why do we only recognize the super-bubbly kind, the ones who can get up in front of a crowd, talk impressively and be outgoing? Some of us are super-shy, who don't ever talk in front of people, and think there's something wrong with us. We *need* people like that. We need quiet, intellectual, thinking, emotional people who maybe get depressed once in a while and then get super-giggly.

But we don't understand that when we have a gift – part of our personality – along with it comes a negative; you don't get one without the other. I tend to be impulsive and a procrastinator. I may have a lot of work to do but I say to my wife: "Let's go out to dinner", or I'll buy her a rose, well, a carnation, okay, I'll pick her a couple of dandelions, and bring them to her. I'm impulsive, and she loves that. But along with that she gets the disorganized part of me that puts things off to the last minute. I go on a trip leaving fifteen things for her to do that I forgot about. She gets one side of me; she gets the other.

Some mothers are unbelievable housekeepers, but the only problem with that is they drive you *crazy*. It's like you're living in a hospital! Walk around the house and she's behind you with a spray, saying: "Don't touch that!" And so your room looks like an absolute disaster area – you've found more creative ways to stuff clothes than anyone I know . . . The rest of the place looks spotless, so when friends come over you know the house is going to look great!

Other parents aren't that tidy. The entire house looks like a tornado hit it, and when people want to come over you don't want them to. If you get one good characteristic – that they don't really care how the house looks and they don't bug you about it – then you also get the other, which is when your friends come over they go, "Sheesh! We're going to go to a movie . . ."

You get one, you get the other. If my wife wants me organized I can adjust a little bit, I can become more organized, but I'll never be Mr Organized because once I become that I lose my impulsiveness, which she likes (I think).

The Church needs *all* of us. It needs the quiet and shy as well as the emotionally unstable, those who are super-high one day and super-down the next. Tony Campolo is the most hyper guy I've ever seen. When he's speaking he can spit further than anyone I know! But I've been with him in his dark moments. Tony's so high and energetic, but when he gets depressed, we're talking major depression. That's what you get, an incredible, intense, unbelievable guy with all this energy, who every once in a while totally crashes and burns.

For some of us it's hormonal. Some girls get depressed once a month and, you know, the answer is not to pray about it, God's not going to make you a guy! Some are pre-menstrual two weeks and post-menstrual the other two – there's three days a year when you're really great!! That's a gift from God, I think. . . . We need all of those kind of things working together in the Church and learn to be happy about our uniqueness.

It's time that we as Christians began to focus on the reality and presence of Jesus, and to fall in love with him. Too many Christians today are into all kinds of theological weird stuff. They're Charismatic, they're Not Charismatic, they're into this, they're into that.

It's about time we began to focus on the centre of our faith, and that's the living Christ. And if we begin to do that instead of focusing on the little idiosyncracies that make us different, I believe the oneness and unity that will come across will make such a difference to the world.

C. S. Lewis – that great American theologian who attended Jimmy Swaggart Bible College – said some great things about the Church. The Church is the one place where, when you walk in the door, you discover people there who ordinarily would never get along, who can't stand each other and argue politics all the way out to the car. But once they're in church the unity of their fellowship in Christ is able, not so much to get rid of those differences – it just means those differences don't matter at that particular moment and we can all worship together.

There's a false oneness, a false unity, permeating our churches today, saying, don't ever question or criticize or say something's wrong, because pointing to problems creates disunity and dissent in the Church. That's not true – you're trying to help fix it and make unity happen. We all need to focus on that centre, the total reality of Jesus Christ.

The American author Walter Wangerin Jnr, who's a Lutheran minister in Evansville, Indiana, has written a great book called *Ragman*. See if this makes the point I've been raising.

Even before the dawn one Friday morning I notice a young man, handsome and strong, walking the alleys of our city. He was pulling an old cart filled with clothes both bright and new, and he was calling in a clear, tenor voice: "Rags!" Ah, the air was foul and the first light filthy to be crossed by such sweet music.

"Rags! New rags for old! I take your tired rags! Rags!"

"Now, this is a wonder," I thought to myself, for the man stood six-feet-four, and his arms were like tree limbs, hard and muscular, and his eyes flashed intelligence. Could he find no better job than this, to be a ragman in the inner city?

I followed him. My curiosity drove me. And I wasn't disappointed.

Soon the ragman saw a woman sitting on her back porch. She was sobbing into a handkerchief, sighing, and shedding a thousand tears. Her knees and elbows made a sad X. Her shoulders shook. Her heart was breaking.

The ragman stopped his cart. Quietly, he walked to the woman, stepping round tin cans, dead toys, and Pampers.

"Give me your rag," he said so gently, "and I'll give you another."

He slipped the handkerchief from her eyes. She looked up, and he laid across her palm a linen cloth so clean and new that it shone. She blinked from the gift to the giver.

Then, as he began to pull his cart again, the ragman did a strange thing; he put her stained handkerchief to his own face; and then *he* began to weep, to sob as grievously as she had done, his shoulders shaking. Yet she was left without a tear.

"This *is* a wonder", I breathed to myself, and I followed the sobbing ragman like a child who cannot turn away from mystery.

"Rags! Rags! New rags for old!"

In a little while, when the sky showed grey behind the rooftops and I could see the shredded curtains hanging out of black windows, the ragman came upon a girl whose head was wrapped in a bandage, whose eyes were empty. Blood soaked her bandage. A single line of blood ran down her cheek.

Now the tall ragman looked upon this child with pity, and he drew a lovely yellow bonnet from his cart.

"Give me your rag," he said tracing his own line on her cheek, "and I'll give you mine."

The child could only gaze at him while he loosened the bandage, removed it, and tied it to his own head. The bonnet he set on hers. And I gasped at what I saw, for with the bandage went the wound! Against his brow it ran a darker, more substantial blood – his own!

"Rags! Rags! I take old rags!" cried the sobbing, bleeding, strong, intelligent ragman.

The sun hurt both the sky, now, and my eyes; the ragman seemed more and more to hurry.

"Are you going to work?" he asked a man who leaned against a telephone pole. The man shook his head.

The ragman pressed him: "Do you have a job?"

"Are you crazy?" sneered the other. He pulled away from the pole, revealing the right sleeve of his jacket – flat, the cuff stuffed into the pocket. He had no arm.

"So," said the ragman, "give me your jacket, and I'll give you mine."

Such quiet authority in his voice!

The one-armed man took off his jacket. So did the ragman – and I trembled at what I saw: for the ragman's arm stayed in its sleeve, and when the other put it on he had two good arms, thick as tree limbs; but the ragman had only one.

"Go to work," he said.

After that he found a drunk, lying unconscious beneath an army blanket, an old man, hunched, wizened and sick. He took that blanket and wrapped it around himself, but for the drunk he left new clothes.

And now I had to run to keep up with the ragman. Though he was weeping uncontrollably, and bleeding freely at the forehead, pulling his cart with one arm, stumbling for drunkenness, falling again and again, exhausted, old, old, and sick, yet he went with terrible speed. On spider's legs he skittered through the alleys of the city, this mile and the next, until he came to its limits, and then he rushed beyond.

I wept to see the change in this man. I hurt to see his sorrow. And yet I needed to see where he was going in such haste, perhaps to know what drove him so.

The little old ragman – he came to a landfill. He came to the garbage pits. And then I wanted to help him in what he did, but I hung back, hiding. He climbed a hill. With tormented labour he cleared a little space on that hill. Then he sighed. He lay down. He pillowed his head on a handkerchief and a jacket. He covered his bones with an army blanket. And he died.

Oh, how I cried to witness that death! I slumped in a junked car and wailed and mourned as one who has no hope – because I had come to love the ragman. Every other face had faded in the wonder of this man, and I cherished him; but he died. I sobbed myself to sleep.

I did not know – how could I know? – that I slept through Friday night and Saturday and its night, too.

But then, on Sunday morning, I was wakened by a violence.

Light – pure, hard, demanding light – slammed against my sour face, and I looked, and I saw the last and the first wonder of all. There was the ragman, folding the blanket most carefully, a scar on his forehead, but alive! And, besides that, healthy! There was no sign of sorrow, nor of age, and all the rags that he had gathered shone for cleanliness.

Well, then I lowered my head and, trembling for all that I had seen, I myself walked up to the ragman. I told him my name with shame, for I was a sorry figure next to him. Then I took off all my clothes in that place, and I said to him with deep yearning in my voice: "Dress me."

He dressed me. My Lord, he put new rags on me, and I am a wonder beside him. The ragman, the ragman, the Christ!

* * *

That's the Jesus we need to proclaim to this world, the one who takes all of our clothes and disposes of them and gives us new rags. That's our message; that's our unity; that's our hope.

May God help all of us to be the kind of Christians who communicate that Jesus to this world.

2

God and the Unclear Family

A friend just out of theological college once had a wild experience in his church. It was time for the children's sermon, which, let's face it, is the only part of a service adults understand. He asked a bunch of kids sitting around him at the front of the church: "What's grey, has big bushy hair and four legs?" They just stared at him. Feeling embarrassed, he asked another question: "What's grey, has bushy hair and runs up and down trees?" More silence. "Okay. What has four legs, thick bushy grey hair, runs up and down trees, gathers nuts, then hides them?" A boy in the back raised his hand and said: "I know the answer's supposed to be Jesus, but it sounds like a squirrel to me."

Don't you feel when you go to church or attend a Christian conference that you're supposed to give the *right* answer, you know, *the* religious answer? When we tell stories to children we conclude with truths like: "The Bible is a road map", then pull out a gigantic map and say, "If you want to get to one place you have to go through the Bible to find it". Afterwards the children sit around, puzzled, having had no idea what you were on about, whereas their parents are all wearing light bulbs: "*Now* I finally understand the Bible!" Then when we finally get old enough to understand object lessons we quit using them.

Let's check out Acts 3 verses 1–10, the story of Peter and John:

One day Peter and John were going up to the temple at the time of prayer – at three in the afternoon. Now a man crippled from birth was being carried to the temple gate called Beautiful, where he was put every day to beg from those going to the temple courts. When he saw Peter and John about to enter, he asked them for money (*sounds like a TV evangelist*). Peter looked straight at him, as did John. Then Peter said: "Look at us!" So the man gave them his attention, expecting to get something from them.

Then Peter said: "Silver or gold I do not have, but what I have I give you. In the name of Jesus Christ of Nazareth, walk." Taking him by the right hand, he helped him up, and instantly the man's feet and ankles became strong. He jumped to his feet and began to walk. Then he went with them into the temple courts, walking and jumping, and praising God. When all the people saw him walking and praising God, they recognized him as the same man who used to sit begging at the temple gate called Beautiful, and they were all filled with wonder and amazement at what had happened to him.

Let's see how we can apply this passage to ourselves and our families. There are two categories of people here: the first, the crippled man, who had got into a daily routine that robbed him of any expectations about his life. That's very easy to do. Many Christians have allowed their faith and lives to be robbed of any life whatsoever.

The theologian Frederick Buechner says: "Be very careful of familiar scripture because familiar scripture has no impact on us at all." When I need to remember something I write a little note and stick it to the bathroom mirror the evening before, to remind me the next day. Next morning I don't see the note; it's right in front of me but I don't recognize it because it has become part of the landscape. Many people's lives have become routine. When I ask kids what they think of when they think of adults, they answer: *"Boring!"* They're right. Somewhere along the way we give up with life. That's why it's a shame games are wasted on the young. Little kids who play hide-and-seek are OK at it, fifty-year-olds (like me) would *love* to play it. Wouldn't you love to tell all your adult neighbours late at night: "We're going to play hide-and-seek"? Now that I'm older I know some unbelievably great places to hide, but I can't play any more. That's the paradox: once we finally learn how to live life, we quit living.

Back in the biblical story, we see a man crippled from birth. Because of this he comes to the same spot every day, but without any expectations. He'd go and be very comfortable in his crippledness, coming to the exact same place and expecting the exact same thing to happen in his life. And that's exactly what happened. The same old thing, the same friends, the same spot, everything was the same.

Routines rob us of the expectations and spontaniety that life has to offer. In our families there are many ways to fall into routines. See if any of the following sound familiar:

"I start taking my wife or husband for granted." We assume our partner is there, that s/he knows I really care about him/her. One of the first places we fall into a routine is when we take each other for granted. Then we never affirm each other; we just keep on living and nothing ever happens.

Men tend to be macho and can't say affectionate, tender things to their wife or kids. When's the last time you wrote your wife a note to say how much you love her? You could hide the note under her pillow, in the microwave, in the rubbish . . .

Children, when did you last tell your parents you love them? Or even put a little note saying that in the middle of your dirty clothes? One teenage girl I know did that. She had a gigantic heap of dirty clothes in her bedroom, and on top of it she put a note that read: "Mum, I know I always leave my dirty clothes around, but I want you to know how much I love you and how much I appreciate the fact that you do my laundry." She came home from school that afternoon to find her mum sitting on the clothes, crying. She was convinced her daughter was pregnant – why else would she write a note like that?

We get into such a routine way of living we never realize that we never tell our partner, who we're with every single day of our lives: "You're incredible. You've got to be incredible to live with me so long. You're beautiful, your gorgeous, you have the most incredible gifts." And we don't say that enough to our children either.

It's remarkably easy to get into a routine of never telling our children anything positive, when all we do is talk about the negatives. Recently I returned from a trip to find my two college-age boys had cleaned up the entire house so thoroughly it looked like a hospital. I couldn't believe it! I knew they'd thrown a party while we were gone – why else would it be this clean? It was immaculate. When I walked in they were hanging around, obviously expecting me to gasp: "Wow! Look at this place. It's unbelievable!"

Instead I walked straight downstairs into their bedroom (which looked like a tornado had just left) and said: "Nice job on the room, guys. You can't even clean up your room while I'm gone." Later my daughter told me I'd devastated them. They were upset for I hadn't even noticed what they had done; all I could do was yell about what they hadn't.

Sometimes we are so caught up in the little routines of our lives we miss the glorious and special things our children do for us. You come home after a hard day's work, your daughter has drawn a great little picture which she excitedly hands to you, and you dismiss it with a casual: "Yeah, great. I'm busy". You completely miss this beautiful moment you could have had with your child.

The crippled man got into a routine; so do we. We often see our children as an interruption and prefer them to watch television because it stops them from bugging us. "Isn't there something on television?" we ask them. A bad soap comes on with its neon glow and we yell: "Get that thing off!" Children have a knack of interrupting our lives and the routines we've fallen into.

I've one son in his mid-twenties and another just finished college. I'll never forget the day I sent my son off to college. As he began walking off I realized: "I'm done, finished. Whatever he's going to be, he'll be." It happened so quickly. Twenty-two years and he's gone in ten seconds. As I said goodbye to him I had tears in my eyes: he turned around, saw me crying and started running for he felt embarrassed by my behaviour.

Children grow up so fast. One day, BOOM!, they're gone. So take time to tell them how much you love them. And don't ever take those around you for granted.

What is it about us in the West? We don't affirm anyone by telling them how great they are. Once while speaking to a bunch of 15- to 18-year-old high school kids at a camp I wondered when I would lose their attention, when they'd yawn, look at their watches and mutter: "I wonder when this will be over?" Yet after that meeting a shy girl came up to me and said: "I just wanted to say that I like you."

I couldn't believe it! I began crying in front of her for I was so moved by what she had said. She could have said she liked my talk, but that wouldn't have made the same impression. Little things like what that girl said to me will change people's lives, and help give them the strength to face another day. Even I'm willing to look in the mirror one more day when someone says that to me. I know what a difference it makes in my life, and I don't think we affirm people enough.

We lose our dreams and our vision. Many adults have already given up; they're into the routines of life, there's no hope any more so they settle for simply existing, living out their days with retirement as the Holy Grail they're not even particularly bothered about. Even the young don't have any dreams or a vision either. People stuck in a routine quickly lose all their expectations about life – they don't really expect anything exciting will happen. So many teenagers are really fifty, sixty, seventy years old inside; they give up. What a tragedy.

South of where we live in California is Mexico. Often we take a group of people across the border, go live in a dump for a week and build houses for the poor. One time I told my church about it and afterwards a seventy-five-year-old lady walked up to me – it took her about fifteen minutes to get there – and said: "I want to go to Mexico!" I told her there was no electricity, no showers, nothing. She said no problem, as long as I could get a doctor to come down. I couldn't believe it – a seventy-five-year-old lady wanting to build a house in Mexico! Maybe it'll take her an hour to hammer a nail in, but she'll do it. And I thought about how this woman had lost neither the joy nor the expectations of life.

We also lose our spontaneity. One thing that makes Christians Christian is that we are spontaneous people; we always do what we are not expected to do. That's the great thing about Jesus, and why he ended up on the cross; everybody expected the Messiah to live a certain way but he didn't live any of the ways expected of him. And that's what I like about Christian people; we don't do things the way people are supposed to – we're surprising people. That's also what I love about Church – you can always expect it to be a wild and crazy place.

Can you imagine being in church one Sunday morning and the pastor says something to which you respond: "YEAH!! Right!" Wouldn't it be great if in the middle of your pastor's sermon you stood up and said: "Excuse me. I don't have any idea what you're talking about. Could you explain it to me again?" I love that kind of spontaneity.

Remember how in the passage the crippled man

was lying there with no expectations, he'd totally given up and was used to being where he was? Incidentally, many people like being depressed. When life deals them a rough blow, they get into a situation where they really like it. This man had been ill for thirty-eight years; he'd been lying by the pool waiting for someone to throw him in – nobody did. Jesus walked up to him and the first thing he asked was: "Do you want to get well?" His disciples were probably saying: "That's a tough question. We can see why he's the Messiah . . . Of course he wants to get well!"

Maybe he didn't. Maybe he liked being where he was for he was used to being around the same people and he really enjoyed that. And Jesus figured that out right away – that many people *like* being ill and get comfortable being where they are. That man didn't want to take the risk change would require. Sometimes people locked in a routine need to be shaken up a bit.

I love doing that in sermons. When I see someone dozing off – his name is Dan – I yell: "And then DAN . . ." and he sits bolt upright while I keep on going. God sometimes has to do this to get our attention, just as in the story of Peter and John talking to a crippled man. He asked them for money, they replied they had none and that they only had Jesus. If he wanted to walk again they'd take care of that. And healed him right then and there.

Peter and John could have ignored the man, but they didn't. They listened to what he had to say: then didn't give him what he wanted – money – but rather what he needed. Jesus has the ability to give us what we need, not what we want. Sometimes in America it seems God is simply an extension of what you want. Is that what the Christian faith is really all about? That if you become a Christian you don't get cancer, your girlfriend doesn't get pregnant . . .

Two college kids, a girl and her boyfriend, once came to a youth minister friend of mine in a church in southern California – the weirdo capital of the world – and were very upset because the girl had got pregnant. They were upset not because she was pregnant but because they didn't understand *why* she was pregnant – every time they had sex they prayed to God to prevent her from getting pregnant!

Many people have the same idea about the Christian faith – God is nothing more than an extension of what we want. If you think that, you're wrong. Jesus will never give you what you want, but what you need. Sometimes what we need is what we want, but not very often. Jesus knows what we really need; that's what he gives to us. But – and here's the crunch – if you decide to follow Jesus it'll upset everyone around you.

When the crippled man was healed the Bible says everyone was amazed; they couldn't believe what happened. Many of us have been Christians for so long that nothing amazes us any more. Why? Because after we become Christians we decide our job is to *straighten everybody else out*, to make sure they all live the way they're supposed to – no drinking, no drugs, no ideas. We spend all our time pointing out what sin is, but we don't need to – they already know what it is; what they *don't* know is about forgiveness, about how Jesus frees and liberates them. They haven't heard the good news of the Gospel.

To paraphrase Robert Capon: "Most of us are like ill-taught piano students. When you took piano lessons and went to a recital, as it came your turn to play your solo, you were more worried about making a mistake than about hearing the music."

It's time we understood that the good news of the Gospel is that we are people who have heard the Good News, the music of the grace of God. We should be people who don't run around constantly worrying if we make a mistake. The great news of the Gospel is that everyone knows we make mistakes – and that's my definition of the Church.

I pastor a church for people who don't like going to church and I tell them the Church is a place for sick people. We *know* we're sick; the people out there don't. I've been to churches where I don't think they know that; they act as though visitors inconvenience them. Many people don't go to church, not because Jesus turns them off, but because we Christians have decided to make them feel like outsiders.

Look at Zacchaeus in Luke 19. He was such an unlikely person to have dinner with Jesus. Of all the people you would have thought Jesus would have had dinner with, it would have been religious, powerful and well-known people. Instead, Jesus selected a man who is a traitor to his own people, a man who was super-short, a teeny, tiny guy nobody liked.

It's amazing to think Jesus selected Zachaeus until we realize he loves *us*, that he would have dinner with _____ [insert your name here]. The disciples were all weirdos; nobody wanted to have dinner with any of them either. They never understood what Jesus meant when he kept telling them he was going to die. And then when he was crucified they wailed: "He died!" Really clever.

Knowing that the disciples were a bit slow encourages me.

The same thing happened to Moses. He tended sheep for forty years until one day he came across a gigantic burning bush that wasn't being consumed by fire but had a voice come out of it. And what did Moses say? The Bible says (verbatim): "I must turn aside now and see why this bush doth burn." That's the English translation for the Hebrew word "AAAAGGGHHHHH!!!!"

God spoke to him by name – just as he knows all of us by name. The great thing about the Christian God is that he knows us by name. He told Moses to go to Pharaoh and tell him to let his people go. Moses was so blown away that God wanted him to do this he replied: "I can't. I'm a wimp."

Moses said what we would say, but I think he was also pouting, hoping Robert Schuller was in heaven to yell: "Moses, you can do it. I know you can; just think strong thoughts. Believe in yourself Moses – discover the real you. Go out there and do it!" Moses kept muttering: "I'm a wimp", and God replied: "You're right. However, the issue isn't your wimpiness but that I'm God."

The beauty of the Gospel is that God has chosen the most unlikely people to be in his Kingdom. God knows *exactly* what we are. We haven't fooled him and he says that in spite of all that he has chosen us. The issue isn't God, but us. He's the one who will make the difference.

Our faith is in a living God who loves and wants the most unlikely people to be part of his Kingdom: Us. Notice how Jesus had dinner with Zacchaeus?

Dinner? How dull. But that, again, is the beauty of the Gospel: Jesus comes to us in the ordinariness of our lives and gives us new meaning and new life.

Everything in family life becomes a routine. Dinner's the same old thing every day. Isn't it great that Jesus decided to have an ordinary dinner, and after they'd eaten Zacchaeus said: "I've really blown it. I'm a total phoney who has robbed and cheated people. I'm going to pay them back more than I stole from them."

Jesus then makes this incredible statement: "I have come to seek and to save those who are lost." When you read that you go: "Oh, 'lost', that's a religious word we use all the time . . ." The church organ's playing in the background. Actually, what Jesus really says is: "I have come to seek and to save those who are *in the wrong place*." When we get to know God all that means is we are in the *right* place.

I've always wondered what it meant to know "the will of God". Did God come down and tell me what brand of toothpaste and shirt to buy and who to talk to? There are people this happens to, you know. "I was sitting at home and God told me to go and call Bob." That's never happened to me. I think to be in the will of God is what Jesus said to Zacchaeus. You may not know all the specifics – who you're supposed to marry, what college you're going to go to – but you do understand that where you are *right now* is where you're supposed to be.

You're doing the washing up. You're doing the laundry. This is where you're supposed to be – that's what the Christian faith means; you know that at this particular moment in this particular time of your life, this, generally, is where you're supposed to be. Be satisfied with where you are right now. God has come down to the unlikeliest of people – us – and brought us to his Kingdom. Now, we are where we ought to be.

A priest I know was once in a retreat with a group of nuns. They would all sit around and study the Bible late at night, then go to bed, think about it, get up in the morning, come back together and reflect on what they had thought about and the scripture they'd read. Catherine, one of the nuns, said she had had the most incredible dream. The way she said it, everyone went: "Ohh . . ." She then asked: "Would you like to hear it?" "Yeah!!"

"I was in a huge dance hall along with many beautiful women and gorgeous men. Suddenly the band began to play. The men began selecting women to dance with. All were paired off, except me. I stood there by myself, with all these couples dancing, when the most gorgeous, intense, tall and handsome man I'd ever seen walked into the hall. He looked around, and even the dancers began to notice him. Suddenly he looked straight at me with the most intense and beautiful eyes I'd ever seen.

"He walked straight over to me and asked me to dance. I said, 'Yes', even though I couldn't dance, and he took me in his arms and walked on to the dance floor. It was beautiful. I knew exactly what to do, and we danced all over the floor. We were so good, everybody else stopped to watch us. As we danced I noticed his hands had nail prints in them. We continued to dance, then he suddenly stopped, leaned over to my ear and whispered. 'Catherine, I'm crazy about you.'"

That's the Gospel. Jesus has selected us, out of everyone in the dance hall, and he has taken us in his arms. He whispers in our ear, "_____ [insert your name here], I'm crazy about you."

Isn't that good news? The God of the universe is absolutely, totally crazy about US.

3

Family Matters

I have five kids – at last count – and on Father's Day what normally happens is that they celebrate their father's day. One year, by about 2 p.m., my kids had said nothing. There were no cards, no presents, nothing. I thought I'd at least get breakfast in bed, but there's nothing – everyone's watching television. When I walked in they all said: "Dad, could you get us some breakfast?" "Sure. No problem." So I make them breakfast and the days goes on and I'm waiting for the big surprise. Nothing.

By two o'clock I was furious. I decided I hated kids and never should have had them in the first place. I was upset and communicated this by pouting. I walked around, my kids asked how I'm doing and I yelled: "Fine!"

I got so mad my wife and I went onto the front lawn of our house and I said, trying not to get upset: "These kids are so selfish. They haven't said one thing, I'm sick of them. We're going out to dinner, I don't care what they have – they can have TV dinners, coco puffs – I'm sick of it."

Just then the door opens and my older boys come running out of the house wearing ski masks. They run over and attack me, knock me down on to the ground, tie my arms behind my back, pick me up, throw me in the car, blindfold me and drive off. Half-an-hour later

I've been in four cars and haven't got a clue where I am. They stop, pull me out, sit me up on a chair, whip the blindfold off and lo! I'm back in my own yard. I walked back in, sat down, had my blindfold removed and there in front of me was the table set with linen, china, silver – looking like they'd stolen it from a number of restaurants in the area – and a menu.

It was unbelievable. They'd fixed me all my favourite food, my daughters were dressed like waitresses and my boys had phoney dinner jackets on. They served me an incredible meal and played country music for me 'cos I like that. It was one of the most memorable Father's Days I've ever had. I had no idea; usually they'd give me ties and socks, which I've long forgotten about, but I've never forgotten that Father's Day.

Many family problems start because we give up and aren't creative any more. And we don't put energy into our relationships and our lives. There is no such thing as dating any more. Instead you find out from a friend if this person likes you and then you call her up – after you already know she likes you – and ask if she wants to go out. And then you don't even go out; you just want to know if she's going, if she would go.

One girl told me that a guy called her up and asked if she'd like to go out. "Yeah." "Where would you like to go?" he asked. "I don't know." "You want to go out to a movie or something like that?" "No." "You want to go out for dinner?" "No." "Do you want to come over and visit me?" "No." "I just want to know if you'd go with me." She said, exasperated: "We never had a date. He just called me up and asked, 'Are we still going together?'

Hey, we've having a fun time – this is great . . ."

People aren't very creative when they go out these days. There're so many great things to do and no one does them. Males are so uncreative. We're so macho it's like: "You wanna go out?" "Yeah." "Where do you wanna go?" "I don't know." "How about a movie?" "Naw. I don't wanna go to a movie." "Anything else?" "No." "Well, guess it's McDonald's then."

I've talked to many girls who have said they'd give anything for a guy to call them up and ask: "Do you want to go on a picnic? We'll go to the park and have a picnic lunch – it'll be fantastic!" In response the guys say: "Yeah, right, give me a break", but the truth is there's no creativity.

Once my son asked me: "Dad, I've got this great idea for a date. Would you rent a big giant truck for me to take to a drive-in? I want you to take the truck there and park it in the back."

I think this is ridiculous. "Yeah. OK son, fine." But he told me what he wanted me to do. He wanted me to set up this date where I parked the truck at the back of a drive-in movie site with the rear end facing the screen. Then I leave. Night – and movie – time comes. Everybody's parked and watching the movie, then about half-way through my son says: "Let's go get something to eat." They walk back to the snack shop in the middle of the drive-in but keep going all the way to the back where the truck is. When they get there there's a table set with china and crystal glass, a friend dressed in a dinner jacket stands there and serves an incredible meal while they're watching the movie. He told me the only thing missing was his waterbed . . .

What a really creative fun idea! There isn't enough of that going on in the family. These days there are so many seminars on how to get on with your mum and dad, and how to be a good parent, that we get so *serious* about good parenting and lose the idea of having fun in the family. And some people's families don't even know how to *spell* F–U–N.

Let's face it. Many adults are boring. It's time for us all to stop going through all this spiritual honour-your-father stuff – learn how to have fun with your parents instead! When you come home say: "Hey, Mum and Dad, let's go play hide-and-seek. You both go down to the park and hide, and we'll stay here with the keg of beer . . ."

It's really important to have fun. The game *Pictionary* is great to draw and play with your parents, though when they start losing they'll say: "OK, that's it. Time's up, you lose." "What do you mean we lose?" "I'm your parent, that's why. Just do it."

Now, a story: "It will strengthen your relationship." That was the advice Lori gave to Tina. Lori had been in a similar situation with her boyfriend. They had been going steady for a long time. Their relationship was shaky, and having sex seemed to bring the two of them closer together. She would strongly recommend that to Tina.

Mark, Tina's boyfriend, had been talking to her for the past three months about having sex. Tina knew that if she didn't have sex with Mark they would break up very soon. She was confused and didn't know what to do. Andy, Lori's boyfriend, had been urging Mark to have sex with Tina. Mark and Tina had been going steady for nearly a year, and he had even mentioned to Andy that he might marry Tina some day. They were that serious and still not having sex. Andy could not understand it.

Tina had decided. She knew she love Mark very much. After having sex with him she wrote three pages in her diary about their new relationship. Lori was right. Having sex with Mark did bring them closer together.

Tina's mother was furious. She'd found Tina's diary while cleaning her room and had read it. Tina couldn't believe it. Her mother told her never to see Mark again.

That's the situation. Now take a few minutes to list the five characters from the best to absolute scumbag, to show the sort of issues we need to confront. Then write down the order you have come up with, and why.

Now some people say Andy was the worst because he was interfering. Others think they were all scumbags; Mark and Tina were the worst, because they shouldn't have listened to anybody. Mum was the worst . . . One thing to notice is how some people think Mum is the worst and put her at the top; others put her at the bottom or somewhere in between. Here is evidence of the expectations we put on our parents, where they fit in and what our value system is. But doesn't the Bible have a lot to say about parenting? It does, although there're a lot of arguments over what those verses mean.

I don't want to get into a big theological treatise here, but instead want to be as practical as possible. The following is a list for parents:

Parenting is overrated. All the years I've been at church it has always been understood that if your kids turn out screwed up it's all your fault. If your kids are messed up, you were doing something *in the dark*: something's going on in your house that no one else knows about. But surely we all know anyway that there's a whole lot going on in our own homes that we don't know about.

Children sometimes turn out the way they do without Mum and Dad having done anything wrong. I don't know why and neither do psychologists. I've talked to parents whose first kid was no problem. Come their second, and it's unbelievable. They raise the child the same way, but the kid turns out radically different. I think there's genetic stuff going on we don't know about, but everything our kids turn out to be isn't necessarily because we, as parents, totally messed up and did something horribly wrong.

All children are radically different, which is wonderful. That's what's so great about kids; the more you have, the more your genes go bananas with the mixes they come up with. That's beautiful. But problems occur when parents *want* all their children to be alike – for the second to be like the first.

The second is *never* like the first. We all worry about the first child, waking up forty times during the night because we're so concerned about it. The next one arrives and it's: "You go and get the child, I'm not getting him. I changed the nappies yesterday . . . c'mon!" No wonder the elder child is always the one taking charge.

Parents don't do this deliberately; they just can't

help it. I've five children, so now I never see a nappy –
I get the others to change it. That's the way it is. Each
kid grows up differently.

Besides, different parents do different things well.
When you get in a room with a bunch of parents you
get intimidated because other parents do what you
don't do well, like cleaning the house. Some have
their house smelling of pine and as clean as a hospital,
with rooms people only sit in once a year. Others are
so messy they never seem to get in order. Maybe
that's because you have five children. As you clean it
they're dirtying it behind your back. It's said they
never finish painting San Francisco's Golden Gate
bridge; the same goes for our house. You never finish
cleaning it – with a bunch of kids it just keeps getting
messier.

Stop being intimidated by what others do better
than you do. Now I don't like to take my kids
camping. So they don't know how to fish, hunt, dig a
latrine – not even how to put up a tent. As I travel
about three months a year, I don't see my children
every day like other people do. So I do different
things like, for example, not allowing school to get in
the way of my kids' education. When I'm home and
want to spend time with them, I take them out of
school because I want them to know our relationship
is more important than that particular school day.

I have never yet written a serious note for my kids
to excuse them the day off school. Teachers get
totally frustrated – "I'm sorry my kids didn't come
to school but their favourite cartoons were on."
Colombia's the drug capital of the world, and one of
my boys was absent from school for three days once

so I wrote a note: "I'm sorry my son wasn't here, but he had to take a trip down to South America and was detained for a couple of days at the border." He's now at a foster home . . .

Another time my high-school son forgot his packed lunch one day, so I took it in a brown paper bag, attached a little teddy bear to it and asked them to deliver it to his class. He's travelling around India now . . .

I believe that kind of attitude and joy is something I can do – maybe you couldn't, your child would end up in gaol! Whatever it is, we all have something we can do really well. Some of us are great at making clothes; others are incredible mechanics – there's something that not only am I unable to do, but my kids have inherited the inability. I can't fix anything. I can take anything and put it in backwards, upside-down and reverse the wiring.

We needn't get intimidated by others who do things differently. Each of us has gifts unique to us, and if that's not what your parents do well, great. They'll still have something they do well, like sleep. Be boring – now that's a real gift.

Another thing to understand about parents is that they can't be natural with their own kids. It's impossible. My son walked in from high school with his best friend Kirk. Kirk said: "Hi, Mr Yaconelli." "Kirk, how're you doing?" "Terrible." "What's the matter?" I asked. "I just flunked my French test." "That's not a big deal. You're a bright kid. You'll get an 'A' and that'll average it up to a 'C'. You'll be OK. Don't worry about it." As he walks out of the door he says to my son: "Your dad is great! Mine would yell and scream at me, but your dad's a cool guy."

A week later my son arrives from school. "Hi, Dad." "Hi, son. How're you doing?" "Not very good." "What's the matter?" "I just flunked my English test." I said: "You're on restriction for a week." He answered: "What? Kirk comes over and you're Mr Nice Guy, Mr Understanding. I come home and I'm on restriction for a week!" "I'll tell you why. I don't care if Kirk's an idiot; my kid's not going to be one."

If my daughter walks in tomorrow and says: "Dad, I'm pregnant", I'm not going to say: "Really? Well let's sit down and look at our options." I'm going to do what any dad would do – scream!

That's why parents can't be neutral with their children. When you're having a discussion or you're talking about anything that really matters, your parents are going to freak totally and interrupt you. They'll stop you, be too intense and smother you because they love you too much. They're too close to you; they're your own flesh and blood. That's why you need neutral adults, like grandparents.

You row with your mother, your grandfather intervenes, talks to her, then comes out, pats you on the head and helps you pack your bags. Seriously, he provides a buffer zone. That's why there are youth workers and people who work in the Church. Young people need neutral adults they can go to and say: "My mum and dad are driving me crazy." You can't do that to your own parents; they can't handle that. So, realize that your parents love you so much they're unable to be neutral about you. It's that simple.

Parents also get into a routine where they never have anything positive to say to you. That's so destructive.

Everyone is special and unique; we parents know that, though we seldom say it, but find negative things, so instead of telling our kids how beautiful they are we yell: "Did you brush your teeth?" The result is we need to write them a note.

A few Thanksgivings ago I wrote a letter to each one of my children telling them all the things about them that were really great. Each letter was different, and each one specifically talked about a gift — for example, I have a daughter who had cancer when she was two years old; she's now nineteen going on twenty-five. In her note I wrote: "You are so special because you weren't supposed to be here. You know that, and so you know it's easy to get to me. You've got that little twinkle in your eye and you know that when you look at me in a particular way I'm dead meat. That's a unique and special gift."

Now and again my daughter looks at me and goes: "Hey, dad . . ." She didn't know she had that great way about her, and often we parents, who *know* their greatest gifts — may have to look a while: "Dear son, you have the most incredible ability to hide dirty clothes in your bedroom."

Parents are good at forgetting to hug our kids. I know when they're fifteen, sixteen and seventeen they're going: "Yeeugghh!!" I don't care whether my kids stiffen up like that; I'm going to hug them anyway. In fact, if they do that I hang around their high school, and when I see them walking across campus I yell: "LISA!!" Now they let me hug them all the time, no problem.

Young people have told me a lot of things they wish their parents did. One is what I've already discussed, to let them know they're loved. That means you have to say: "I love you." Write it down. Don't just hug them. Let them know you love them. Don't assume that just because you're there they already know that. And show them affection.

The other thing is genuineness, which is more than being consistent; it means being true to who you are. You may be an emotional yo-yo; maybe you're inconsistent and that's your consistency. Sometimes we parents try hard to be what we're not. Just be the person you are. Do that and your kids will appreciate it. Too many parents run around trying to act like teenagers. It only ends up in grief, for children end up competing with their mums and dads – your mum's trying to look as young as you.

Parents just need to be parents. So your weight begins to shift and muscle tone goes when you get older. My children know that. Now when we go to the beach it's great; I can walk on there with my umbrella and little picnic basket, my street shoes and black socks. Then my children ask me to guard the other end of the beach, but that's OK, for I'm getting older and can learn to deal with that.

Young people today want guidance. They don't want a dictatorial tell-me-what-to-do; they want to work it out with you. They want to sit down and discuss things, but it's hard to talk with your parents about the things that really matter, like sex education.

As a parent I found it so hard to talk about sex. Once I sat down with my boys and it was the worst experience I've ever had. "Well guys, it's time to talk about sex. Let's talk about masturbation. You guys have any problem with that?" "NO!!" "Any questions?" "NO!!!" Then I ask: "What is it?"

We assume that just because everybody talks about sex, and our children see sex everywhere, they're getting sex education. They're not. They need to hear what their parents think about it. I don't care how difficult it is or how much trouble you have; it's worthwhile. Children want to know what their parents' value are, what they believe and what they think. We parents assume they know, just because they live in our house. They don't know, nor do they really understand what you believe and why you believe it. The more you can share that the better off you'll be.

However, often children aren't ready to talk about things when you are. I've heard religious speakers say that one of the most important things you can do in a family is to have devotions with your family every night. I don't do that. I tried once, but they just sat there saying nothing until I yelled: "But the Bible's good for you!!"

Three days later as I worked underneath the car on the transmission, my eldest child slid under the car and asked: "Dad, what is the Trinity like?" I replied: "Why didn't you want to talk about this three nights ago?" So I left the car and talked to him about the Trinity. Sometimes our children have questions at the most unbelievable times, like two or three o'clock in the morning. When they want to talk, we parents ought to take advantage of those special moments, whenever they are, instead of trying to force significant conversations to happen.

Parents have to learn to let go of their children.

We've got to let them grow up and give them privacy – not an inner sanctum that parents can never enter – for they need their secrets. They need secrets when they're young; that's part of growing up. Then when they grow up they're willing to trust somebody to tell those secrets to. You also need to let them be silent once in a while, and admit if you make mistakes.

Now kids, when's the last time you wrote your parents a note saying: "I just wanted to let you know what a great mum and dad you are before I leave, for Bob and I are eloping . . ."?

And finally, children need to feel that their parents are trying to understand them. I don't understand about all their culture and what's going on, but that's fine; if I at least try to understand them, the real them, the one they're struggling with, that'll make such an incredible difference to their lives.

The American writer Walt Wangerin Jnr wrote a story about his eight-year-old son's experience with super-itchy poison ivy. He lay in bed covered in Fell's Napther soap, a thick soap that makes you look like a mummy. It's to keep your skin from moving so you won't get itchy and scratch it. Read on:

> My dad came in, we had a talk. It was a nice talk; he's a kind man. I didn't move or look at him, but I could hear his voice. Now there are certain places on a boy's body which, try as he might, he can't keep still. On that place on my body there was at that time one poison ivy dot, and that bodily part began to move, so that that single poison ivy dot began to itch.
>
> This was more than I could take. In a moment

all the plans of the world and all the remedies failed. Life was very bleak.

Without turning my head, without so much as a sob or a moan, I began to cry. The tears trailed down my temple and pooled in my ear. I thought I would die soon.

And then I heard a strangled sound to my left. It was my father. He'd risen to his feet. His hands were up in the air and empty. His face was so full of anguish seeing my tears, that my own heart went out to the man. He turned fully around in the room, seeming so helpless, and then he bolted for the door, yelling, "Calamine lotion!"

I was experienced in the ways of poison ivy. I knew that calamine lotion was utterly useless, even if it could get to my rash. But my rash was covered by a rind of Fell's Napter soap. It was no good; no good at all.

Nevertheless, when my father appeared again with a giant bottle of calamine lotion, when my father knelt down beside the bed, uncovered me and began so gently with his own hand to rub it on, when my father's eyes, damp with the tears of suffering, so that I saw with wonder that my pain had actually become his own pain, and that it was our pain that had sent him rocketing to the drug store, when I saw and felt that miracle a second miracle took place. The ivy did not itch.

Calamine lotion did not do this thing. My father's love did this thing, and I knew it. Oh my heart ached to have such a father, who could enter into me and hurt so much he took my hurt away.

Young people today need those kind of parents, who do everything they can to take the hurt away from adolescence and growing up. The more we can do that – even if we make many mistakes – our children will understand and love us. And they'll turn out fine. It may take them years, but they'll get there.

4

Jimmy and Me

Jorge Rodriguez was a famous Mexican bank robber in the early 1900s. He would sneak across the border, rob banks in Texas, then return to Mexico. He always evaded capture; that is, until a Texas ranger resolved to stop him. So, one night, when a lone horseman was seen sneaking back across the Rio Grande to Mexico, the ranger knew it must be Jorge because of the moneybags on the horse's back.

The ranger followed him across the border to a small town, watched him dismount and walk into a cantina. Both guns ready, he barged through the door, and saw Jorge having a drink at a table. The ranger yelled at him: "Jorge, if you don't tell me where you've hidden the money from all the bank robberies I'm going to blow you away!"

But there was a slight problem. Jorge couldn't understand English. However, a man at the bar could, and he offered to translate. He then told Jorge exactly what the Texas ranger had said. Jorge, in deep shock, then blurted out to the translator where he had hidden the proceeds from his many bank robberies. The translator looked up at the ranger, shrugged his shoulders and said: "Jorge is a very brave man. He is not afraid to die."

Something got lost in the translation! TV evangelists are the same. The American culture permits and encourages these people to flourish for some peculiar reason. Indeed, the following illustration may help put things in perspective. When *The Last Temptation of Christ* – the movie many people weren't happy about and haven't seen – was released in 1988 a fundamentalist called R. L. Hymers (fundamentalists don't have first names, only initials) staged a protest about it. He got some people to go to Universal Studios and wave protest signs. Then he persuaded a man from his church to dress up like Jesus, carry a giant cross on his back and walk to the film company.

Of course the media, always in search of a photo opportunity and some religious crackpot controversy for the evening news, heard about this and sent camera crews and reporters over. When R. L. Hymers saw the phalanx of photographers, he made Jesus lie on the ground on top of the cross and hammered a couple of nails into him. Just as he was about to read a prepared statement regarding *The Last Temptation of Christ* his Jesus began to moan and groan in pain (he was a method actor) and R.L.'s statement went unheard because Jesus moaned too loudly. Finally R.L. stopped and yelled: "Will you shut up a minute?" Later, as I watched this debacle on television, I thought about how he hadn't figured out how to handle the media.

With regard to the medium of television there're many questions we haven't asked or been willing to talk about. Now you don't sell something if people don't want it; the reason TV evangelists do so well is because, for some reason, some people want what they are selling. Many Americans feel they have little or no value and no idea at all about what to do with their lives. I'm convinced most people don't realize they can make a difference, that their life *does* matter.

So why do they watch and support TV evangelists? Because they see someone they believe to be an incredibly important person doing incredibly important things. They then think that by watching and basking in the cold glow of the neon tube, and by supporting these people, they somehow assume some of their significance and importance.

It's easy to watch television and see someone talking about the Gospel. That's the easiest part of being a Christian – you just sit there, watch them and agree with them. Indeed, the fastest growing churches are those where the preacher has an overhead projector. He tells us what the original Greek and Hebrew meant, while we all sit around feeling dumb and thinking, "But I don't know any Greek . . .". We're made to feel insignificant because this person is up there pontificating, but that's OK for it means we don't have to study the Bible, just listen.

TV evangelism is selfish. You can sit in the comfort of your own home and watch an evangelist. All you have to do is send in a few dollars and for that you get a free Bible – a free Jerry Falwell Bible with his picture on the front, which is not a real bargain . . . Almost all the gift giving that goes on is nothing more than you purchasing something; it's very, very selfish. You sit there, watch, send in money – a thousand dollars, for instance, would at one point enable you to stay at the Heritage Hotel for a week a year for the rest of your life.

TV evangelism is successful. Well, look at the TV evangelists; they all have the successful look – make-up, super-neat hair and they drive limousines. Have you ever wondered how people can give money to evangelists who drive around in limos and have jet planes? Because, when they see that it makes *them* feel successful. Many of us feel we haven't done anything that matters, that we've never really succeeded in anything. When we see someone who has and we feel we're supporting them, we take on some of that success ourselves. It's tragic.

TV evangelism is also successful because we refuse to take technology seriously. The sociologist Jacques Ellul says technology isn't neutral, that it alters, changes and affects our lives so that we'll never be the same. Once you take the Gospel and put it on television you change and alter it – it'll never be the Gospel it once was. It gets distorted.

Technology changes things. Think about church buildings; they're not a sin, but neither are they neutral – the moment you buy one you're in big trouble because now you've got to pay for it. You end up serving the building instead of the building serving you. When it comes to technology the moment you try to condense the Gospel to make it fit television's parameters – no programmes longer than an hour, always looking at the cameras – you change and alter the message in such a way that no longer is it the Gospel.

Technology always wins. The moment you compromise and start using technology, eventually it'll get you. Have you ever thought how ridiculous it is to watch the weather reports after the News? "Fifty-three degrees, sorry, eighteen celsius, and yesterday it was seventeen celsius", and we go: "Wow!! Eighteen, then it was seventeen, OK!" Who cares? It's absolute trivia brought to us by satellite technology. Television so warps and controls our view of reality that it takes us over. The notion of "Christian" television is nonsense; it's like having a "Christian" motorcycle — what does it do, aside from making a lot of noise? It certainly doesn't make good television.

If you're ugly or overweight, then I'm sorry, but you've been disqualified from becoming a TV evangelist. That fact alone immediately distorts our view of the Gospel. TV and rock stars are all super-thin, and we sit there figuring we'll never make TV evangelists or rock singers. Television distorts our view of who makes a good Christian and who doesn't. That disturbs and upsets me, for that makes us feel inadequate, thinking that Jesus doesn't have anything to say to us if we're ugly and don't look good. What nonsense!

I wish we knew what the disciples looked like, though I bet they were the most motley looking group you'd ever see. Now I find *that* encouraging because I feel I can fit in to that, whereas I can't fit in to television.

Television is entertainment. In order to make us watch it it must be entertaining. But the Gospel isn't very entertaining; neither is Jesus. To have to make the Gospel entertaining tells me that something's wrong.

Technology requires an absence rather than a presence. Instead of my showing you my personality I have to give up my personality in order for it to work. It's like McDonald's. When I travel from New York to London I can expect to eat the same Big Mac in both cities. Everything about it is identical. That's what technology does – it's the great leveller, removing any spontaneity from any of us. The more we use it, the more we lose who we are and become somebody different.

We don't need anything that reduces us further. Instead we need something that makes us more present, that allows our personalities and uniqueness to distinguish themselves. That's why artists and intellectuals have never fitted into churches. Intellectuals are always a pain in the arm; they always ask questions. After you've done three ways to overcome depression, nine ways to have a happy marriage, six ways to know the will of God, they'll ask: "But isn't there a seventh?"

And artists are weird for they are emotional yo-yos. What's wrong with that? So they get depressed easily. When you get depressed in the Church everybody acts like there's something wrong with you. They always ask: "What's the matter?" "I'm depressed." Then they look at you and offer the following encouraging words: "Don't be depressed." It's as though you're an idiot! You don't give somebody who's depressed a Robert Schuller tape on *Eight Ways to Overcome Depression*, but rather the Bible says when they get depressed you get depressed with them.

Good artists are people who, in the midst of their depression, produce good music and poetry; that's where that gift of their art comes from. Forty or fifty per cent of the great artists in history all went over the edge. Artists are on the line; that's a gift. We eliminate all kinds of people when we worship technology and allow it to take over.

The Church refuses to take evil seriously. We always blow it by constantly making the wrong things – drinking, smoking, drugs – evil. Those are obvious – anybody knows that – but it seems the Church is always giving the rules to the world – "No drinking. No drugs. No smoking!!" The trouble is the Church keeps making issues out of the wrong things, so the things that really *do* make a difference are never talked about. And Evil is one of them. The *Friday the 13th* and *A Nightmare on Elm Street* series of films, for instance, trivialize evil until we don't take it seriously any more. And one of the most evil things in our culture is Power.

What we do to TV evangelists is give them lots of power. When you give people power they tend to misuse it. We do it to our ministers and they love it. We allow them to speak in a monologue as no one speaks in the entire universe, and to dress up in a silly robe. Haven't you ever wished that one Sunday your pastor would stand up in the pulpit and say: "I've just had one heck of a fight with my wife . . . I really don't have anything to say because I'm so wiped out over this argument. Why don't you folks take the service this morning?"

Wouldn't it be great? Though if it happened every Sunday then maybe there would be a problem.

We like to give people power and the trappings of power. But it taints and affects them and will eventually, if we're not careful, drain them of all personal worth. Power should not be given to people flippantly. Be very careful. Many ministers think everything they say is the truth and God-given, so when they're home they exercise the same lack of discrimination — "Clean up your room. God told me you need to do that now." That's why they need to have people around them who can say: "That's a load of rubbish."

That's the biggest problem with Robert Schuller, and even with Billy Graham, whom I love and respect (and he's the only one I do, to be honest). They get surrounded by Yes-people. A big-time evangelical in the United States once told me how he had sacrificed his career in business. I told him: "There's one thing you didn't give up that you got instead of money — power."

Power is much more than money, believe me. Money corrupts all of us, and we have left these people, who get all this money, totally unaccountable. There's a church in California — where else? — where on a Sunday morning there were four thousand people in it, and the minister got up and said, "It's time for our new tithing programme", and new tithe cards — called "God's Ninety-day Guarantee Plan" — were passed out to everyone present.

Here's how it works. Everyone was supposed to sign the pledge cards saying they would give ten per cent of their money to the church for the next ninety days. Then after ninety days if you weren't completely satisfied with the result the church would give you your money back. You know what? All four thousand signed the cards. Why didn't they all stand up and go, "What? Are you nuts?" I don't remember Jesus saying, "Take up your cross and follow me, and if within ninety days you're not completely satisfied I'll give you your money back."

The fact is that today people in the Church – you and me – are afraid to argue with the people in power. We're afraid to hold people accountable; we're afraid to create a disturbance; we're afraid to ask the tough questions about where that money is going. It's much easier not to ask any questions and just hope and pray that it's being taken care of, and if it isn't, that God will take care of it later.

But God has given us the power to do that. We are the ones that are accountable. When we give our money we're the ones that ought to be accountable and want to know where that money goes, and if we don't know where it's going then we ought to ask some petty tough questions.

Frankly, the reason these evangelists have been able to dupe people by raising all that money is because the people who support them refuse to ask the tough question and won't go to the board and raise the issues that need raising.

Giving, in TV evangelist terms, is not really giving anything; you give £75, you get £75-worth of merchandise back. That's not giving; we don't understand what giving is today. In my church we don't believe in passing the plate, for that makes people give who maybe don't want to. I want to leave the responsibility for giving in the person's lap so that they have to think about it and remember it themselves.

The trouble in the Church today is that we're taking all the responsibility away from people. My church has a philosophy called "If you don't do it, it doesn't get done". It's simple; if nobody signs up to help in the nursery all the kids come into church.

After one day it's amazing how many people God has spoken to . . .

People have no way of knowing that their life means something if they don't let it not mean anything. You've got to allow the consequences of your not choosing to do something to work themselves out. If nobody wants to teach Sunday school you don't have it; if nobody wants to do what needs to be done, you don't let it be done. People will eventually see that if they don't do it it isn't going to get done, and then they have to take on that accountability and responsibility. In the Church we're robbing many people of living out the consequences of what they're doing.

Fame, like Money and Power, corrupts. Have you ever noticed how rock stars don't sing, but talk? That makes me mad, paying £20 to have a rock star talk to me. People who sing ought to sing; that's their gift. But because we give them so much fame and so much sway over us when they speak we sit there and go "Wow! Amy Grant just said . . ." If anybody else had said it we'd have said, "What rubbish is this?" (nothing personal Amy, but you know what I mean).

What irritates me about rock singers is they tell us about the song – "Here's a song about depression. One day I was really depressed and God really spoke to me, so I'd like to sing this little song which talks about what God was doing in the midst of my depression" – and then they sing, "One day I was depressed . . ." and you think, "Why don't you just sing the song? If you're going to tell us about it, don't sing it; if you're going to sing it you don't need to tell us about it. We'll figure it out."

We *give* these people this position. We like to look at people who are famous and these TV evangelists become famous people. And the moment that happens they lose touch with reality. We like them to be famous and give them a position they really shouldn't have. Fame is a very corrupting influence on us all.

I want to point out two other things we don't understand. In Sodom and Gomorrah the sin wasn't sodomy, but that the people there no longer thought that sodomy was a sin. They were unable to see, understand and define sin any longer. The reason we're into all this TV evangelism stuff is because we're so affected by our culture we can't even tell what's wrong with it. We don't even know how to fix it any longer. We're not able to define what sin is and what it is doing to us – how it is slowly destroying us and robbing us of any sense of what is right and what is wrong.

One thing that bothers me about Jimmy Swaggart is the way he handled telling the public what he did. He got up in front of those television cameras and apologized. That show – I call it a show – made me so mad. Can you imagine what must have been going on in the director's booth – "There's a woman crying. OK, zoom in on those tears. Good close-up. Jimmy's crying. Get his wife, she's right there."

That is just evil. Manipulating television, trying to get the best shot – that's one thing that irritated me about Swaggart's apology. The other thing is that he acted as though saying sorry was enough. But it made great television. Ninety per cent of the people I talked to who watched him apologize were moved by it, saying they really respected how he got up there and apologized, for at least he was honest – unlike Jim Bakker. Even the people in Swaggart's church gave him fifteen standing ovations for sinning. Things have changed somewhere along the way. People used to be stoned; now we give them standing ovations.

But it was only later as we sat in our living rooms and began to think about what we had seen that we began to get madder and madder because we realized that we had been taken to the cleaners. And that's what Swaggart didn't count on; that people would begin to think. The trouble with television is that it keeps you from thinking, and when you finally turn the thing off at last you're able to think. I think that's the biggest issue facing churches today – they need to be the places where they teach us *how to think*. The trouble is, for many of us, we go to church and leave our brains outside; we don't think any more.

Besides, saying you're sorry isn't enough. In America Christianity has become so sentimentalized that repentance is brushed aside. That's what bothers me about Jimmy Swaggart. He doesn't even understand how powerful his own medium, television, is or what he has done to us. He has enjoyed the fact that he has got all this money and his own dynasty – now that he *does* understand – but what he doesn't understand is that he has screwed up the rest of my life.

Everywhere I go, when I tell people I'm a Christian I have to put an asterisk by it – which is hard to do when I'm talking to somebody. I have to say to people: "I'm a Christian, but I'm not like Jimmy Swaggart", and distance myself from him. Do they understand what he's done? His behaviour has made us so cynical that we can't trust anyone, even when we want to. He doesn't have any understanding about what he has done to us. Look what he has done to women; look what he has even done to his wife — what humiliation she must have gone through.

How could Swaggart get back in the pulpit after three months? I'm not saying he's not forgiven — of course he's forgiven, we're all capable of sexual immorality — but he hasn't yet understood repentance. He hasn't understood how long it takes to learn the lessons of his past and the consequences of sin, how long it takes to deal with that and with what he has done in terms of our misunderstanding what the Gospel is really about.

That's what frightens me most about television.

5

The American Daydream

Some people don't believe it's possible to be both a Christian and an American. However, you must realize from the outset that Americans understand everything – including our Christian faith and our whole life and the way we live – solely in terms of performance.

Everything is based on *what you do*, and for Americans that's a big deal. When we meet the first thing we ask is: "What do you do?", because if we can figure out what you do we figure that somehow we know you. The most common term for sexual intercourse in America is "do it" because that's all sex is in America. When you're done you ask your partner: "How was it?" It's a performance, and you simply measure your performance on previous relationships and those relationships to come.

If you realize that you'll understand why American Christians are the way they are. They have to perform in order for them to be accepted as far as God is concerned. And in America if you're not first, you're last; if you don't win, you're nobody. The actor Paul Newman is a motor-racing fanatic and has even driven in the Le Mans 24-hour race. Asked if he ever enjoyed losing he's reputed to have said: "Show me someone who enjoys losing and I'll show you a loser." That's the attitude I mean.

When people give testimonies about what Jesus means in their lives, they spin fantastic and amazing yarns – "I used to be a Hell's Angel. I murdered, raped and plundered. Then I was employed by the Mafia as a freelance hitman. I murdered twenty people and during this time became an alcholic and cocaine addict. I was caught, sentenced to 800 years in jail – reduced to 400 for good behaviour – and became a Christian in Alcatraz. But I got released on a technicality – a miracle! – so here I am today! Isn't God great?!" Like sheep we bleat: "Wah, amazing!" It would be boring if I got up and said: "Hi, I'm Mike. I got average grades at school, I'm a nerd, I do the laundry most of the time at home and I ride a bike. That's me, and I love Jesus. OK."

There's no reason why that shouldn't happen all the time in America, but there you have to be an ex-something – an ex-beauty queen, an ex-football player, an ex-businessman – and have something horrible lurking in your past, something that distinguished you and made you special. The idea that you're special, just the way you are, that you as an individual have unique gifts which make you part of the Kingdom of God, is foreign to us.

Americans are really good at feeling guilty; we have incredible guilt – that's how we are able to manipulate everybody all the time. We use guilt, especially in the Church. If you're feeling really down and go to church, by the end of the sermon you're more depressed than when you went in . . .

Many of us get depressed for we feel we always have to perform – to put on an act – and to keep doing better. Speakers would come to my youth group and say: "Every month I take my family camping." I would immediately feel guilty, because I don't. I hate to camp. That's not something I do, but I always feel like I should do it, because this guy said that's what he did. And I would feel bad about my Christian faith.

Billy Graham has said that he prays for an hour every morning. I don't. Once I felt so guilty that I made out a giant list – my parents, brothers and sisters, uncles and aunts, all the countries in the world, missionaries, everything – then got the stopwatch out and prayed like crazy. Two minutes later, I'm done.

I was convinced God was up in Heaven saying: "Two minutes? Ha, ha, ha, ha, ha, that's it, you're history!" What I didn't understand was that the opposite was happening, that when I finished my two minutes of prayer God was up in Heaven yelling: "You're not going to believe this! Yaconelli just prayed for *two minutes*!!" They're having a pizza party up there and going crazy! God gets excited about the two minutes we gave instead of lecturing us about the fifty-eight minutes we didn't.

Many Americans don't understand that concept. They don't realize that part of our Christian faith is not just this constant performance, always trying to be better, always trying to do well, always having to feel guilty about what I'm *not* doing instead of celebrating what I am.

I love the story of the woman with the blood disease who tried to get to Jesus. I can see the disciples acting like his bodyguards, saying to the crowd: "Out of the way, this is Jesus, the big time guy, with his white robe and glow on his head." Meanwhile, organ music plays in the background. Suddenly a woman thinks if she can only touch Jesus's garment without anyone noticing, she'll get better. The Bible says she reached up and touched his garment, and immediately Jesus stopped. The disciples see this and think he's about to say something, so they yell: "Stand back! This is Jesus – he says great stuff!!" (this is the Revised Yaconelli translation).

Jesus turns and asks: "Who touched me?" and points to the healed woman. Now that is the heart of the Gospel; we matter so much to Jesus that even when we touch his garment anonymously he hears us, stops and takes time to recognize us individually, not because of our performance, but because of our need.

We Americans have a lot to learn about that for we are so performance– , outward– , showy-orientated. And Christians tend to fake it just a little bit; we always have a big smile on our face. Ever met Christians who act like they're on drugs for Jesus? They really bother me. I know they're sincere, but everything is "Praise the Lord!" – "My car broke down. Praise God! I just broke my arm. Praise God!" Now, when I broke my arm "Praise God!" were not the first two words that came to mind.

It's great to be so positive, but it's as if Christians can't ever admit they're human; we can't ever admit we're normal. You ever had a giant fight with your wife on the way to church? As you're pulling into the car park, the pastor comes over and you say: "Hi pastor. Praise God!" Why do we have to be so phoney and pretend so much? Because we've bought the idea that the Christian faith is a performance; it's a show we have to put on.

Putting on a show does more harm than good to the Gospel. When we pretend about the Christian faith, people question if it's real. It's only when we are honest about our faith that it makes any difference. Unfortunately we don't restrict our show-business to the Church, and try to make people who aren't Christians perform too. If someone swears in our presence we tut-tut and say: "Excuse me, I'm a Christian. Do not use that word in my presence."

You say, but Mike, we're Christians and we want to be a witness to that fact. Yeah, fine, but what's the point of doing something like that? Why are you doing that? What are you trying to say to that person? You antagonize them and get their backs up for the wrong reason. God isn't prudish. And he also doesn't want us to pretend and perform, but to be real. Believe it or not, God loves and appreciates us without our having to perform and thereby somehow win his approval.

American Christians are also into *success*. We always have to feel better about ourselves, always competing to show we really are Number One Christians. Have you ever noticed how, when you're depressed, people come up to you and tell you not to be, like you're an idiot? Many people want others to think that by being successful that means they're OK. These same people spend so little time with their children that they're always making excuses for them – "He gives me a lot of trouble but he's really a good kid" – saying they are selfish but great, some kind of "good" selfishness.

We always have to be achieving, to be the best, to be right at the top, and in America that's a big deal. One of the great things about the Church is that all of us are growing, and growth is weird. Remember when you were a teenager? The only way you knew you were growing was when you went to your grandmother's house. Growth is a very slow process, and others notice it before we do. We don't know we're growing; it's just that suddenly people notice that we're different. And you can't manipulate or speed it up.

Americans are into weekend conferences on marriage or one-day seminars on how to be successful. Give me a break. You're going to iron out all your marriage problems in a weekend? Jesus never said: "Three ways to overcome depression . . . three ways to have a happy marriage . . . six ways to know the will of God . . ." He always did the opposite; he would make some obscure statement or tell a parable nobody understood, and that was it. Goodnight.

That's the great truth about the fact that we're constantly growing and changing – we never really know where we are. Part of that process is God trying to wean us; it's tough for both weaner and weanie. Let me illustrate: when I was teaching my kids to walk I didn't do what a lot of churches do – I didn't pick up my kid and then let him go, where he'd walk two steps and fall flat on his face. What I did was I held him up, let him go, then stood behind him. My job was not to keep him from falling but to ensure his fall wasn't fatal. That's what we're doing all the time. Hopefully what the Church means is people around us to ensure that fall isn't fatal.

For so many people, the moment we fall we're out of the Church. Isn't that weird? You go to church on a Sunday morning and you're asked: "How was your week?" "Terrible. I got drunk last night." They then go: "Did you just use the 'D' word? That's it. You're out of here."

Instead people ought to say: "I know what you mean. I've done that myself. I love you very much but you've got to stop", and then hug us and love us and support us, and help us back up on our feet again. But we often feel afraid to be honest and say what we've really done because we're afraid we won't measure up to some kind of success ethic.

Americans are speaker-orientated people, so when we hear Amy Grant or even me tell these great stories we mutter: "Gee, that's never happened to me." Well, it probably never happened to them either. When we tell a story we tend to forget details and it's so easy to say a throwaway line: "And five years later he came to know Jesus." That's very easy to say in one second, but it's not that simple while you're wading through those five years.

I admire Billy Graham – but what do I know about him? I used to think Elizabeth Taylor was the most beautiful woman in the world until I found out she had haemorrhoids. The fact is I don't know what goes on in Billy Graham's life; I compare what I don't know about him to what I do know about me. If he walked into his house and ate a lousy meal, would he say, "Thank you Jesus for this meal, and thanks, Honey, for preparing it, it was great"? I've a feeling he'd do what we do, yell: "What is this? I'm on the road doing crusades – can't I have a decent meal when I'm here?" Now I happen to think Billy Graham is probably a human being with faults and idiosyncracies like the rest of us, and that if you really got to know him you'd probably find out he has got all kinds of weird things wrong with him.

I studied for a while at L'Abri in Switzerland when its founder, the philosopher and theologian Francis Schaeffer, was still alive. He was a special person, and once I travelled with him; his luggage got lost at the airport and the man who wrote *The God who is there* exploded in frustration and anger. God wasn't in the baggage claim department that day, I'll tell you that. It totally blew my image.

We've all had experiences like that. We know ourselves so well, and we don't know these people; we tend to compare what we know of ourselves with what we don't know of them, and that's what creates the problem.

The third thing about the American Church and Christians in general is that *we take ourselves so seriously*. That's why, when I make fun of somebody in the satirical magazine *The Door*, people call it blasphemy. We take Christianity so seriously that many of us have lost the passion and ability to enjoy our faith and have fun.

Americans are serious people; they're constantly uptight. Have you ever been in church when somebody burped, and all the adults fight to keep a straight face? Wouldn't it be great if the pastor stopped the service and said: "All right, who did it?" Why can't we enjoy life? Why can't we relax instead of being so uptight about our faith? It ought to be enjoyable and festive. You can take humour too far and hurt people, but there ought to be that kind of light-heartedness about ourselves, where we never take ourselves so seriously we can't admit it when we blow it.

The beauty of the Gospel is that we're able to nudge each other and have a twinkle in our eye that lets everyone know we don't take ourselves *that* seriously, that we can mess up and still be human beings.

The fourth point about the Christian faith in America is that *we have objectified everyone* – we treat people as things. When you get to this point a number of things happen:

Christians don't listen to each other any longer. The way we communicate our faith is by the fact we don't dance, we don't drink . . . sorry, I was looking at my Baptist notes . . . How do people know I'm a Christian? Is it because I'm some incredibly perfect human being living an incredibly moral life? I'm convinced that what has the most to do with it is that I listen to people. I keep my mouth shut. Too many Christians talk too much. We've too many books, tapes, seminars and speakers blabbing about the Christian faith, and many Christians wish the people responsible for producing all this stuff would shut up long enough to listen.

A friend lost three of his children to cancer. When his last son was dying in hospital every Christian who came in brought either a book or a tape, or else some advice and interpretations of scripture about why God was doing this and allowing it to happen. He said he could hardly wait for them to leave the room. Later a friend of his whose son had been killed in a car accident walked in. He said he never wanted that guy to leave, for he simply grasped his hand and never said a word. We've lost that gift – we don't listen to people any more. We just keep talking, talking, talking and never hear what they have to say.

We don't empathize any more. Americans don't know how to empathize. If you're depressed I offer advice and cheer you up; if that doesn't work I leave the room and send you a tape later. I try to do something quick, to fix it in a hurry because I don't want to be around you while you sit there being depressed; I want to fix it *now*!

Empathy is learning how to feel like that person feels. I once met a forty-five-year-old woman who hadn't been to church since she was a young girl. She told me that when she was twelve years old her parents went to a very liberal church – it was boring, she hated it and didn't want to go – and her dad taught Sunday school there. One Sunday she asked if she could go to a charismatic church down the street with a girlfriend. He said OK, so she went and said it was the most exciting service she had ever attended.

Afterwards she was so excited she forgot her father's Sunday school class was still on and she barged into the church. Everyone turned around and glared at her. Realizing what she had done, she panicked, then got angry. She yelled: "You people are a bunch of hypocrites! You don't even believe in God! Those people in the church down the street know what they're talking about." The congregation turned to look at her father, waiting for him to tell her to shut up. Suddenly she remembered him and saw he had sat down, tears welling up in his eyes. She knew he understood.

We need people who understand like that. All of us are sick and tired of people pointing fingers at us and telling us what we're doing wrong. If somebody would just care enough, care about what we go through, hear us, listen to us, empathize and understand, there'd be a revival. People would start taking Christianity seriously.

We don't stick it out with people long enough. Some people, maybe your parents, Sunday school teacher or minister, may have no idea you're a Christian because they gave up on you years ago. Indeed, this generation of young people will not come to Christ because I tell them to, or because the Church tells them they'd better or else they're going to go to Hell. That used to work; it doesn't any more.

The only way young people will know the truth of the Gospel is if we stick it out with them for the long haul. We need to hang in there with them and persevere and be their friends. The 1979 film *The Great Santini* is set in 1962 and centres round a typical military father (the great Robert Duvall) who was a redneck, saw everything in black and white, and would get his kids up at 4 a.m. to have inspection. Can you imagine? As the movie continues you hate this guy but realize he really does love his kids. One night he arrives home totally drunk, walks into the kitchen and hits his wife. His children hear the commotion and run downstairs. His seventeen-year-old eldest son throws his father against the wall and tells him to leave their mother alone.

Dad storms out and leaves. Their mother goes

upstairs and tells the seventeen-year-old to go out and find him. "Find him? I hate him. I wish you'd get a divorce for I can't stand him. I can't believe you'd ask me to do that. I'm not doing it", he replies. She says: "Yes you are. You love him and I love him, so go find him."

He finds his dad in a drunken stupor, lying beside a tree, mumbling in his drunkenness. His son hears him talk about how his father treated him when he was young. Suddenly the boy understands why his dad is the way he is. He throws his arms around him and tells him: "Dad, I love you, let's go home." Instead of being grateful his dad stands up, tries to hit him and tells him to leave him alone. This happens several times, so the boy starts taunting him by whispering: "Dad, I love you. C'mon, stop me from loving you." Father chases son, and, finally catching up with him, they throw their arms around each other in a wonderful embrace.

As I watched this I thought, that's the Gospel, that's the Good News of what Jesus does with us, and that's what we do with other people. We just stand behind them and taunt them with his love. Just as there's nothing anyone can do to stop Jesus from loving us, there ought to be nothing that keeps us from loving people. That's how we communicate Jesus to this world.

Finally, **accommodation**, which means I do whatever I have to do to meet your needs; I do whatever is required of me to somehow let you know how much I care about you. That's why we minister to the poor – not to put John 3:16 on their house, not to fix their house and then sit them down and tell them about the

Gospel. No. When you have a need I run to meet that need; that's accommodation. I accommodate that need and try to fix it. Whatever your need happens to be, if you're depressed, if you're alone, lonely, stressed out, whatever, I draw alongside you as a Christian. That takes time and effort and requires a great deal of sacrifice. To be honest, many of us aren't willing to do that.

Dr Richard Seltzer has written a wonderful book called *Mortal Lessons*. He's not a Christian, just a surgeon, but if I ever have to be operated on I want him to do it. He's the most unbelievable human I've ever come across and he has written this great story.

Picture this: a beautiful twenty-two-year-old girl who has been married about a year notices a growth on her face and undergoes a biopsy. It's cancer. The doctor warns her there's a chance the facial nerve may be cut during the operation, resulting in that side of her face losing its muscle tone, leaving her face lopsided for the rest of her life. Surgery goes ahead, and Dr Seltzer takes us into the post-operating room. Here's what he describes.

I stand by the bed where a young woman lies. Her face post-operative, her mouth twisted in palsy, clownish. A tiny twig of the facial nerve, the one next to the muscles of her mouth, had been severed. She would be thus from now on. The surgeon had followed with religious fervour the curve of her flesh, I promise you that. Nevertheless, to remove the tumour in her cheek I had cut the little nerve.

Her young husband is in the room. He stands on the other side of the bed and together they seem to dwell on the evening lamplight, isolated from me, private. Who are they? I ask myself, he and this wry mouth I have made, who gaze at and touch each other so generously, greedily. The young woman speaks. "Will my mouth always be like this?" she asks. "Yes," I say, "it will. It's because the nerve was cut."

She nods and is silent. But the young man smiles. "I like it", he says. "It's kind of cute." All at once I know who he is. I understand and I lower my gaze. One is not bold in an encounter with a god. Unmindful, he bends to kiss her crooked mouth and I'm so close I can see how he twists his own lips to accommodate to hers, to show her that her kiss still works.

The Jesus of the Bible is the one who twisted his own body on the cross to tell us we still work. That's the Gospel; that's accommodation, and the world desperately needs to hear that Good News.

6

Backs to the Future

Once upon a time in a decade far, far away a sociologist called Alvin Toffler wrote an excellent book called *Future Shock*. Unfortunately, because that decade in the mists of time was the seventies, no one reads it any more. This is a shame for you should, because Toffler's thesis was how it's not just that things are changing, but that change itself has changed.

When we think of adolescence today, it isn't that kids are accelerated versions of what they were ten years ago – young people are more radical and totally different than in any previous generation. They can't be compared to when their parents were kids; indeed, they're not like they were even several years ago.

So what are these differences and what are the pressures that make today's kids the way they are? When we either think about raising children or look at our own kids, when we look at those around us, what has changed and made them so different? It used to be that when you were young you could be young; now, you can't even *look* young – you wear designer jeans at two or three years old.

Adults pressurize their children to hurry up and grow up to be an adult, instead of allowing them to enjoy being fifteen years old. Let's face it; adults are boring. Why then do we tell kids to grow up and be like us?

The following is a list of things American kids worry about nowadays:

★ if boys kiss their girlfriends too much they'll get mononeucleosis;

★ while making out they should be saying things like "Oh baby";

★ in a long kiss they'll have to breathe through their nose, which will be stuffed up;

★ their breath smells and they've got b.o. and everyone's in on the joke but them;

★ there's a right way to dress and they don't know it;

★ there's a right way to kiss and they don't know it;

★ their date can tell they don't know it;

★ if you're a girl, that you won't have breasts;

★ if you're a guy, that you will;

★ their nose is too fat or too long, their neck is too fat and whether their ears stick out;

★ if they're a boy, whether they'll ever be able to grow a moustache;

★ if they're a girl, worry that they will;

★ and when they go to the bathroom people will hear.

Young people today are under a tremendous amount of pressure to hurry up and get a job, to be successful and get good grades. I think they ought to take a year off once they finish school, and go relax and travel around. Adults should do the same because most of us have no idea what our gifts are or what we want to be; we just hang around, for we've never really had the chance to see what we do well. Go to India, Africa, Mexico, South America, go anywhere they need your help and where, when you do things, it really does make a difference. And you'll be different too; you'll realize what you can do and the gifts you have.

Sitting around telling people they can make a difference to the world doesn't make that difference. We must go and be part of it. We need to take a break to figure out what the call of God – something we never talk about any more – is. We need to talk to our children and each other about what it means to hear the call of God in our lives, where we actually hear – and allow – him to call us to do something.

In this pressure-cooker world we need to find ways to relax. Play games. Try "Manhunt", where you make a list of different types of people – somebody over six feet tall, somebody with red hair, somebody that works at McDonalds, somebody who almost died from eating at McDonalds – and have two hours to find them. We played it once and wanted a responsible adult to drive, so we chose Mrs Culp. She was overweight and therefore, to the kids, uncool. So when they saw her car – which was so big it looked like an army tank – they thought: "Oh boy, fifteen miles an hour . . ." Two hours later Mrs Culp drove up to my house with twenty-three kids in – and on – her car. Mrs Culp who, if she had walked down the street kids would walk on the other side to avoid her, was suddenly a hero. That day changed her life.

Young people need to learn how to have that kind of fun again, how to enjoy life, how to relax and turn the pressure off. That's one of the Gospel's ideas – when you know Jesus you're freed from all this oppressive pressure. When Jesus met the woman by the well he liberated her from her past; he removed her burden. That's what he does.

So many people run around under unbelievable pressure – even in the Church, where the pressure can be even greater because now we also have to measure up to being a good Christian.

When I was young and went to Sunday school we always tried to get our teacher upset by asking her embarrassing questions like: "Could you teach us about french kissing?" She'd blush and get flustered, so we'd then say: "C'mon, there's nothing in the Bible about it and we want to know what to do." She'd think for a minute, then look us square in the eye and reply: "If you ever want to know what you're supposed to do and you don't know how to make that decision and whether there's a Bible verse, just ask yourself this question. 'If Jesus was there, would I do it?'"

That if-Jesus-was-there oppressiveness prevents us from doing *anything*. The truth is if Jesus was here we'd have a great time; we would sense his presence here in radical, fun ways that would liberate rather than oppress us. And that's the Good News of the Gospel.

The second characteristic of young people today is *lostness*. I come from a fundamentalist background – I went to Bob Jones University, and was asked to leave – and fundamentalists talk in a weird way. A word like "lost" means those of us in church are "found" and the pagans "out there" – the ones who aren't in church – are the *lost* ones, who have deliberately turned their back on God. It sounded horrible to me. I wish people were like that today, but they're not; nor do they intentionally turn their back on God.

Where I live in California the only issues we worry about are nuclear war and cows. If a cow gets out of a field and you drive into it, it's your fault, according to Californian law. You also have to apologize to the cow. One day I asked somebody in my church how cows got out so often. He said: "Have you ever noticed how they're always eating? They put their head down, look for a little tuft of grass, nibble until it's gone, and repeat this until the only green tuft left in the field is beside the fence. They nibble and finish that, spot another tuft of grass and walk through a hole in the fence to get to it. So it goes on, until they get lost. Cows nibble their way to lostness."

Suddenly I understood what's going on in our culture. People aren't deliberately turning their back on God, they're just nibbling their way away from his Kingdom. Someone whose marriage is falling apart doesn't get up one morning and intentionally think: "I'm not talking to my wife any more. I'm going to see how far away we can get." Each partner nibbles on their respective jobs and what they both have to do; soon they've nibbled themselves away from each other. And six months later they wake up and realize how far away they've got.

When I ask young people on a Wednesday night what they're going to do come Friday evening, ninety-nine per cent reply: "I dunno." I wish they'd say: "I'm going to sin my brains out!" At least I could work with them, but they don't know what they're going to do. Friday comes, they hear there's a party somewhere and they end up getting drunk – they didn't mean to – they never thought about it but they just ended up there. It's not that people today don't want to know God or give their life to Christ, they simply get so busy they're unable to follow Christ.

It's up to us somehow to figure out how to reach this busy generation of people, who would love to know Christ but are so busy they never have the time. Why does the Church, in response to a culture where everybody's busy, figure out how to make them more busy? We can't do that any more! We have to figure out how to reach this generation by getting into the midst of their busy-ness.

Another characteristic of young people is *indifference*. There's nothing more frustrating than talking to an unresponsive group of people. A youth worker friend of mine told some teenagers they ought not to have sex until they get married. When he was finished someone raised his hand and said: "That's a novel idea."

Years ago we had a moral landscape. We could count on society agreeing on certain principles – even if people didn't live them privately. Nowadays there's a moral indifference, nothing is wrong, no one has ethical standards. Recently I read an article on ethics which said how encouraging it was that because there aren't any ethics nowadays people are starting to think about them. Great. They're starting to think that maybe there ought to be things that are right and wrong, but they have no basis upon which to make any kind of decision.

In America today the biggest issue is lying. People

lie like mad, and my kids have developed the most incredible five-stage programmes – they're so good at it they've got it organized. One of them will say: "Dad, there's a party on on Friday night. Can I go?" I reply: "Uh huh, I've heard about that party, I'm a step ahead of you; there's going to be booze there but no parents present. No, you can't go." I win.

Come Friday night he's getting ready to go out and I ask where he's going. "To a show." "OK, but don't go to that party." He returns at midnight and I'm waiting for him. "Hi son, did you go to that party?" First stage: *you deny everything*. He looks me squarely in the eye and says: "Dad, you told me not to go to the party. I didn't go." I reply: "That's funny, because I drove past the house where the party was and your car was parked there."

Second stage: *you admit only what your parents know*. So he looks at me and goes: "Oh man, I totally forgot, I stopped by the party for about two minutes 'cos I had to give Bob Jones back a shirt I'd borrowed from him." "Well, half-an-hour later I drove back from the store and your car was still there." As soon as I'd say that my kids would yell back: "Your car ran out of gas! Your battery's dead!" – and that's exactly what he'd say, "My car was there but I wasn't. I went to get gas to fill it." I counter with: "That's amazing. It must have taken you four hours to fill it because at 11 o'clock when I came back your car was still there."

Now my kid's just lied to me three straight times in a row; but a lie isn't a lie if you don't get caught, and if you do, then the idea is to cut your losses. So he looks at me and goes to the fourth stage: *claim a crisis.* He says: "Dad, I'm going to be totally honest with you. I went to the party, but the reason I went was because Bob Jones has a drinking problem. He didn't want you to know about it and he wanted me to stay and keep him from drinking. That's why I was there." My kid's now become the Mother Teresa of the party circuit.

I finally say: "You're lying through your teeth." Then he does the most effective stage of all, stage five. He asks: "How many time did you drive past the party — three, four, five times? You know what the difference between you and all my other friends are? You don't trust anything I do. Did you have infra-red cameras and bug the place too?" and slams the door.

An hour later his mother and I walk into his room and say: "I'm sorry." We didn't allow ourselves to go out for a week.

Where did these kids pick this up? From Jim Bakker. He went through exactly the same process. Maybe he called my kids. "Weren't you in a hotel with a woman?" "No way. Absolutely not." "We've got records to show you were." "OK, ten minutes." "You were there longer than ten minutes. We've got records showing that too." "Jimmy Swaggart made me do it." He never could come out and say he did it. He went through the exact same stages; so did Oliver North and so did everybody else in Watergate, Irangate, you name it, Ivan Boesky, all of them. Everybody in our culture has that same mentality — it's not wrong unless you get caught.

The result is that today our kids have no moral landscape — none. Even though they may come to church and listen and nod their head in agreement with what you are saying, when they go out to school where their friends are what they practise is a totally different standard from what they agree with on Sunday in church. They're not able to see the connection between their faith and what goes on in real life.

The fourth characteristic of young people is *selfishness*. In modern Christianity people have become so narcissistic – the seventies was the age of narcissism, and once we learned to spell it it was no longer around. Narcissism has become such an integral part of our lives we don't even know what we're doing. It's the value system that judges everything in life in terms of what we can get out of it – what's it going to do for me? So teenagers say, "Sure I'll become a Christian. What's Jesus going to do for me? If he keeps my girlfriend from getting pregnant, I'm in. If he makes sure I get a good job and make lots of money, that's great. I'll follow Jesus, but if it costs me anything, if I have to deny myself anything, forget it, I don't want anything to do with it."

This selfishness is unbelievable. I hope the British don't inherit the American view of Christianity and the Gospel which is, if you love Jesus and follow him then he becomes an extension of your own selfishness. In front of me is a letter sent out by the church youth group of high school kids who are Christians in the States. A girl in the youth group had a serious problem and the group decided to send a letter out to every church in the area asking them for help. Here it is: I've changed the names:

We're members of youth group, probably a lot like yours. We meet every week for Bible study and fun. We're friends at school; we're learning about what it means to be the Church, to be Christians no matter where we are. Anyway, we're writing to tell you about one of our friends, Tessie, who needs our help and yours. Tessie's a member of our youth group; she's on the cross-country track team at school, she's in choir and a good student.

(Right now, along with me, aren't you thinking to yourself, uh oh, cancer, some horrible disaster has happened, her parents have been killed in an accident this is going to be horrible . . . well, let's see what the horrible thing is . . .)

Everybody likes Tessie pretty well. However, she did a really stupid thing not too long ago. She took her parents' car without permission and got in a wreck. She's OK, but there's almost two thousand pounds worth of damage to the car. Tessie has her permit [you have to get a permit before you can get a driver's licence, like the provisional licence in the UK, and you have to drive with it for a year and always drive with an adult] so the insurance wouldn't pay for the damage.

Tessie feels really bad, and she's never done anything like this before. But her parents are making her pay for the whole thing, and now she has to quit sports to get a job and she probably won't be able to go on any of the choir trips. Work is hard to find around here, and she's

looking, but even if she finds a job it'll take
forever to pay off two thousand pounds. Her
whole year is ruined. She might not even be able
to get it paid off before next year, when she'll be
a senior.

We feel bad for her. Will you help us help her?
We're writing every youth group we can think of
and asking two things – (1) write Tessie and tell
her that even though you don't know her you feel
bad for her, and (2) could you take up a little
collection to help Tessie pay her debt?

Write Tessie a letter? I'd love to write Tessie a letter.
I'd love to tell her: "Get a job!" This youth group
suggested the Christian response to Tessie is to help
her get out of the consequences of her mistakes. She
broke the law, stole her folks' car, wrecked it and
should have to pay for it, but her youth group tried
to figure out how to get her out of all that.

Without picking on this youth group, *they think
this is the Christian thing to do.* They think they're
being the body of Christ and that what they're doing
is an extension of what Jesus would have done in that
situation. That's the scary part. They don't even
realize that all they're doing is nothing more than an
extension of the kind of selfishness we create when
we continue to talk about the Gospel like this.

So what should we be doing? How should we
respond to where young people are today? What
should we be saying to them? I believe what's needed
more than anything else is *the process of grounding*;
we need to start from square one with this generation
by firstly, *talking about the process of conversion*

again. We need to go back to our roots and talk to people about inviting Christ into their life, about saying Yes. We've become so cool and sophisticated about witnessing to people, giving them books and tracts, that we've forgotten how to ask somebody if they want to say Yes. The first step is to begin to ask aggressively if people want to know Christ.

We also need *to help people get to know their Bible.* Most people these days are totally New Testament, and very seldom get into the Old Testament. And you wonder why kids have no heroes today – their heroes are only famous people and they don't know of anybody with any real depth. Go into the Old Testament and there're all these incredible people; they loved God so much and when they sinned, they sinned. The really knew how to sin – I like those kind of people, they don't mess around. There was no doubt, no grey area, and you can see the texture and weave of how Christ works in people.

When we talk about love we automatically go to 1 Corinthians 13. Young people have heard it so often it goes in one ear and out the other. Go to the book of Hosea – *now* we can talk about love. God told Hosea to marry a prostitute; that's interesting. I think you'd get a lot of teenage attention, instead of them all sitting around bored. Whenever I do a study on Hosea I send a postcard to all the guys in my youth group two weeks ahead of time, saying: "Dear Bob, Would God want you to marry a prostitute? Find out in two weeks." That night the room is packed, not with kids but their parents wanting to find out what the answer is!

Young people today aren't liberal or conservative –

they're ignorant! They have no idea what the Bible says or means. Why do we only tell little kids the stories of David and Goliath, and Samson and Delilah? We never wait until they are older and able to really understand who these people are. Instead, we stay in the New Testament and talk boring theology all the time. Theology isn't boring if it's put into the life of a person and seen in action in the Old Testament.

Eugene Peterson has written a book called *A Long Obedience in the Same Direction*, and he says: "Young people today need to acquire a taste for grace." This means you can't convince young people not to sin by telling them not to. If you tell them: "The Bible says, 'Thou shalt not sin'", they'll look at you and say: "That's interesting. Maybe I'll think about it", then they go and sin.

The Christian community has to learn to wait for people to acquire a taste for grace. We have to be there when they make mistakes, when they sin and blow it, so we can pick up the pieces and go from there. Our job is to learn to love people through their sin, to be there and then be able to tell them what went on and why. It's very important to be able to do that.

Not long ago I went to a youth meeting where a friend of mine was talking about sex and why you should wait until you got married. Unfortunately he used an analogy that was used when I was a kid to try and convince us. "You can either rent a car or buy one. If you rent a car you don't take care of it because you're going to give it back so what do you care? But if you own a car, then you take care of it. So if you marry somebody and then have sex . . ."

That was the analogy; only when I was a kid and my Sunday school teacher used it we gasped: "That's heavy!" This time, he hadn't even finished when a girl at the back stuck up her hand and asked: "What if you rent a car for a year and then buy it?" The guy's now a used car salesman . . .

He didn't have an answer because young people are different from what they used to be. They'll argue with you, question and push you; they don't accept things because God or you said it. We have to love them into the Kingdom of God, to hang around them for a while before they finally really understand the Gospel. That's our role, and that's the process. But we don't want to wait that long; we want to hurry everybody into the Kingdom of God, *now*! It's not that easy – we've got to wait people out and show patience while they develop what I call "a process of dissatisfaction".

There's a number of ways to do that. For instance, by shattering their illusions; we can use the media – TV, movies, videos – to let them see the folly and nonsense of much of life. But that's not enough; it's no good telling them not to go, instead of realizing they'll go regardless.

We've also got to start talking about the bad news of repentance – and it's not just feeling sorry for what I do, but going a step farther. G. K. Chesterton, a guy who used to work at Burger King near where I live, said: "Christianity hasn't been tried and found wanting; it's been found difficult and left untried." The Christian faith is difficult and we're not saying that enough – we make it seem too easy. We act as though it's so much fun and so exciting; we don't explain the cost of becoming a Christian, and how that price will change your life and last as long as it does.

People need to *celebrate* more. We don't celebrate enough. A friend of mine works with street gangs in Chicago. He started having a Bible study with some gang leaders and one night when walking down a street he saw a gang leader he knew. He yelled: "Hey Bobby! How you doing?" "Fine!" "No, I mean, how are you doing with God?" Bobby looked at him and said: "Pretty good. In fact, this week I'm actually trying to cut down on shooting people."

Can you imagine Bobby getting up in your church on a Sunday morning? "I just want to praise God – this week I only shot three people . . ." People would be outraged and demand he was arrested, but we ought to be helping him celebrate the moves he's making towards God. I'd want him to know how happy I was about the steps he's making towards God, instead of constantly making him feel bad about the steps he *isn't* making. We need to allow people to grow up in their own time.

We need adults who are passionate about Jesus and about life, whose passion overflows into other people's lives. You don't have to be cool or neat, you can be overweight or ugly, you don't have to know your theology and have everything figured out, but if you are passionate about Jesus and life, it overflows. Passion should be part of life – and it's not just because I'm Italian, I can't help it, it's in my genes – for every time people see our lives they wonder: "If you love Jesus so much, if you say this life is so great, then how come you don't act like you're alive?"

Why aren't we passionate about our faith, allowing it to consume us until we really do feel that deep joy? This generation would be a lot closer to Christ if we realized and believed that.

7

Truth, the Holy Truth and Big, Big Lies

Four people are in a private aeroplane at 10,000 feet when the pilot turns around and says: "I have some bad news and some even worse news. The bad news is, the plane is going to crash; the engine has stopped, we've run out of fuel, we're going down. The worse news is there are three parachutes and four of us, and I'm taking one of them. I've three kids and a wife who needs me to support her, so I'll see you later", and he jumps out of the plane.

There're now two parachutes and three people left — a minister and two teenagers, one of whom considers himself the smartest teenager in the world. The smartest teenager in the world says: "I'm taking the next parachute because I'm so smart the world needs me to discover a cure for cancer. Goodbye", and he jumps out the plane.

The old minister and the other teenager are left. The minister tells the teenage boy to take the other parachute because he has lived a long life and will go to be with God. The teenager replies: "Don't worry about it. There are still two parachutes left. The smartest teenager in the world jumped out of the plane with my rucksack."

The whole struggle in the Christian life is to be smart enough to know the difference between a rucksack and a parachute. I am sick of the dishonesty in the Church, and it's easy to get terribly frustrated when, on going to a Christian conference, you attend a seminar where the speaker says: "You're not happy or fulfilled, you're not loving Jesus or seeking first his Kingdom. What's the matter with you?" So you go to the seminar next door and there the speaker says: "You're happy, fulfilled and loving Jesus but why are you not struggling? What's the matter with you?"

Soon your head spins – "I'm OK, I'm not OK" – as speakers trot out the little group of stories they like to tell. They tell their unbelievable experiences until we're moved to tears and laugh. But things like that never happen to *us*. We hear these incredible stories and freak out when a speaker gets up and says: "Last week when I was in Belfast . . ., the week before that when I was in Hungary . . ., I remember being in the Philippines . . ., when I was in Nicaragua . . ."

By now you're going: "Nicaragua? I haven't been to London yet!" We get frustrated for we come to seminars to be encouraged and moved, to hear the truth, and what we get is story after story after story, experience after experience after experience. Well, all the stuff you hear from the platform never happened. Or it certainly didn't happen the way it is being told. When you tell a story, the nature of storytelling is that you leave out some parts, condense others and remember selected juicy parts, then tie them all together with a beginning, a middle and an end.

We hear true stories that are never quite how things happened. It's easy to say in a story: "And then, ten years later, she came back." Meanwhile you're in tears, for your wife left you last year and you

wish that story would happen to you, but you've nine
more years to wait! When we hear a story like that
it's easy to get frustrated. I'm not saying conference
speakers are intentionally dishonest – I sincerely hope
not – but when stories are told and points are made,
reality is manipulated. A slice of reality isn't the
whole story. Listen, enjoy, reflect, but never take it as
literal fact until you've had time to think about it.

A speaker friend of mine actually tells a story about
how his brother got sick and died. Then he makes the
point. One time I said to him: "But your brother's
still alive. I just met him!" and he replied: "Yeah, I
know, but it sounds better when he dies."

We hear a lot of stories whose situations are
manipulated and altered because they make a great
point – a point that is true – but in the process of
listening to those stories we begin to wonder what's
wrong with us. This has created in the Church a sense
of how easy it is to lie.

In America we've done this and created a Church
full of people who think the business of Christianity
is to lie and deceive people about who you are.
There's a great scripture, Matthew 9:9 – and notice
how my writing this makes it sound like I know the
whole Bible by heart, and that I said to myself as
I was putting this chapter together: "Oh yeah,
Matthew, the ninth chapter, the ninth verse . . .
that's a great little verse in there." It's the only one I
know!

The trouble with the Bible is it's printed on paper
and is written in an abstract manner. We don't realize
the exciting stuff that really happened. Meanwhile
back in Matthew 9:9: "As Jesus went on from there,

he saw a man named Matthew sitting at the tax collector's booth. 'Follow me', he told him, and Matthew got up and followed him."

That verse tells us so much. Here was Matthew, an incredibly rich and powerful tax collector, who was hated by his own race of people, but with tremendous powers of manipulation over everyone else. On the outside he looked like an impenetrable power, someone whose path we wouldn't want to cross and who really had his life together. And Jesus, he walks along – his hair is glowing, organ music plays in the background, he wears a white robe and floats through the air (no wonder Matthew followed him); that isn't what happened really – and sees this wealthy tax collector, whom he looks square in the eye and says: "Matthew, follow me", *and he does*!

That tells me that Matthew on the inside was nothing like the Matthew on the outside. Everybody thought he was what he was on the outside, but what they didn't know was that deep inside he was lonely, frustrated, empty, hollow and totally at the end of his rope. Suddenly Jesus comes along and understands that.

On the surface we all appear reasonably well-adjusted, but just beneath the surface is loneliness, heartache and brokenness; our families are falling apart, for our parents are either getting divorced or already have, we've been abused – sexually we're treated like objects – by a partner in a relationship we need to get out of because it's destroying us, we're on drugs, there're all kinds of problems but we don't feel that in the Church, in Christianity, we can be honest about them, that we can really let people know who we are. So we become expert at learning how to deceive each other, to be happy-go-lucky, smiling and looking great all the time. That's what the American culture has done to us. We're treated like we have to be on drugs for Jesus all of the time. Doesn't that bug you about Americans? Be honest. Every time you meet them it's "HHHEEEYYYYYY!!!!!!" plus an additional rib-cracking bear hug. And you're smothered and bemused, thinking: "What is this, does he sell cars? He doesn't even know me . . ."

Some of us like relationships that are a bit deeper than that. But all of us feel Christianity is where we pretend we're something we're not. If the Church is the Church, if the Gospel really is true, then the Church is the one place I can hardly wait to get to because it's the *only* place I don't have to pretend any more, where I can admit I got drunk last night and not have everyone there recoil in horror, but say: "I know what you mean."

It would be wonderful if a minister got up to preach one Sunday morning and told his congregation: "I can't preach today. I got in a giant argument with my wife last night. We started up again this morning and argued all the way here, and that's why she isn't here – she's in the nursery taking care of the kids, she didn't want to hear me. The argument still hasn't been resolved for she hasn't come around to my point of view, which is the correct one, and, basically I'm so wiped out over this that I don't have anything to say." And then sat down.

Just once! Everybody in the congregation would yell and cheer: "He has fights with his wife! Yeahh!! He's just like me!"

It's important that we realize Church – and Christianity – is the place where we can give up pretending and be real, *I can be me*, I can begin to be honest about who I am. The more we can allow for that the greater the impact on the world. The only difference between us and people who don't go to church is that we know we're sick, they don't. So what's impressive about church? Nothing. It's just some sick people who say: "I'm sick, I'm in deep trouble, and that's why I'm here." But when I go to most churches I get the opposite feeling; it's like "What are *you* doing here? You look a little sickly. Let me help you . . . leave." That attitude is noticed and leads people to believe Christianity is for those who pretend they're something they're not.

My wife and I are volunteer leaders in a Wednesday night club for teenagers called "Young Life". There is a little girl there called Clarissa, an adopted Thai with beautiful eyes and who is a real live-wire. At one meeting I noticed she was sitting with a girlfriend, who began to cry. Afterwards I asked her what the matter was. She said Clarissa had told her that last weekend she'd tried to commit suicide.

Later I walked over to Clarissa, who was laughing with friends and having a great time, and said: "How are you?" "Great." "No, how are you *really* doing?" "Oh, really good", she replied. "I understand last weekend you weren't doing so great." I can't explain what happened next, but physiologically that girl changed; she went from happy, smiling and giddy to crying so intensely that tears literally squirted out of her eyes. I was blown away. No one had any idea that just beneath the surface this girl was dying inside, that she was hurting and totally falling apart.

What's wrong with Christianity? We can talk about theological issues but if people like Clarissa can't come near the Gospel and feel, "This is the one place where I can tell you what's really going on inside", then we are all in trouble. Honesty ought to be the fragrance of the Church – a group of people who are honest *and real* – that draws the world to Jesus Christ.

Real honesty and real truth will never totally happen. We won't walk around saying everything we think – "That's an ugly dress; you think that hairdo looks good, think again; you mean you actually got up, looked in the mirror and said you look fine, well I got news for you" – for that's not the kind of honesty I mean. We can be who we are and say what's going on in our lives, and can really describe the people we are. *That* is what will make a difference and what we will communicate.

The other thing we do that makes us feel we can't be honest is that we manipulate scripture. You ask me if I believe in the Bible, and I'll reply, Absolutely. Do I believe it's the word of God? and I say, Yes. All of it? Yeah. But the moment we start reading and quoting scripture we manipulate it.

Acts 12 – another chapter I've memorized by heart – is great because it's about Peter locked in gaol. He has no way of getting out and his local church is praying he'll get out of gaol when, guess what?, an angel shows up, takes Peter from the gaol, sets him in front of its gates, says: "See you later", and leaves. Peter goes to the little church where they're praying and knocks on the door. They finally answer it, look at him and run back in. Later they return and he says: "It's me – the guy you've been praying to get out of gaol – I'm out!" They refuse to believe him because they think he's really an angel. They would rather believe that.

That's what always gets me about people who are into "End Times" theology, you know, that Jesus is coming back and that Russia is the king of the north, America is something else, and the ten-headed beast . . . blah blah blah. We'd rather sit around and get totally freaked out about that stuff than the real life going on around us. The real life was Peter saying: "I'm here, you've been praying for me, but if you keep praying I'm going to be dead because they'll catch me again! Open the door you idiots!"

I don't know how many sermons I've heard preached on this passage, and the conclusion has always been: "If you just pray and believe God, he will answer your prayer." We hear a sermon like that and think: "That's true, that's what happened. I'd better pray a bit harder." The trouble is, they don't tell us the whole story – they leave out the first part of the chapter. Acts 12 begins: "It was about this time that King Herod arrested some who belonged to the church, intending to persecute them. He had James, the brother of John, put to death with the sword."

Now I've haven't heard anyone preach on that . . . This chapter has a 50:50 ratio; if you're Peter, you're happy, but James didn't quite make it – he was killed. Do you think the Church forgot to pray about him? Or maybe they didn't like him – "Lord, help Peter, but James, you know how he is, he wants to be with you anyway." Give me a break! The Church prayed just as hard for James as it did for Peter! Peter got out, James didn't. Not only did Peter get out, but they didn't really believe he'd get out anyway! How's that for believing prayer?

I don't know why Peter got out of gaol. I can't figure it out — and neither could they. They prayed because they had to pray — that's what prayer is, it's taking out petitions before God, it's telling God what's going on in our lives, it's responding to who God is, it's telling him all of our needs and of our gratefulness to him, and it's praying everything we possibly can. Then we sit back and sometimes God comes in and intervenes — and sometimes he doesn't.

But don't anyone ever tell you there's a formula — you pray, this will happen; you do this, this is what will work; three ways to do that; four ways to overcome depression: nine ways to have a happy marriage; six ways to know the will of God — for your life. It's not in the New Testament, but I think that near the end of Jesus's ministry the disciples all got together one night and one of them said: "Don't ask him any more questions. It's worse when you do."

Another pressure that tells us we shouldn't be honest is that we live in a culture so affected by television and the other media, so manipulated by these external things that we begin to romanticize life and believe it is condensed into a sixty-second commercial. The American telephone company AT&T has a one-minute commercial that makes me cry every time I see it. It features a father who hasn't seen his son in twenty years, and you see his son thinking about picking up the phone, then he doesn't

– will he, won't he – until finally he does. When his father's phone rings he is looking at a photograph of his son, he picks up the receiver and hears: "Dad", "Son . . .", and meanwhile I'm bawling my eyes out!

This twenty-year relationship has been repaired in one minute – father and son are back together again. It's the prodigal son, and it's the telephone that fixed it!

We see so much television, so many movies and videos, and read so many magazines we think all of life is like this – that it's all fixed up, solved and resolved, everything is worked out in a few seconds and is all taken care of. We romanticize life like crazy. And we romanticize what the Christian life is about.

On your honeymoon you have a great time, because that's what's supposed to happen. But most couples don't. They lie about their honeymoons, which are terrible because they discover the person they really married – dirty socks, the whole thing. And when they return they can't tell anybody because nobody talks to them because, well, when you're newly married and just back from your honeymoon, what do you do?

My wife and I felt called to, uh, minister in Hawaii, so we left our five kids at home and spent a wonderful week there. On the final night we went to an incredible restaurant right next to the ocean and ordered an absolutely fabulous meal. It had been a week together without kids and we'd had a great time lying around on the beach, making love and catching some rays. The waiter brought the meal – this really happened, I'm not exaggerating this story; OK, it was in Los Angeles, actually it was Des

Moines, Iowa — and as he set it down I was so overwhelmed with love for my wife I started to cry. The waiter asked me if anything was the matter and I said: "No, we've just had a most wonderful evening."

The following year we had to go back to Hawaii again to do God's work. We went back to the same restaurant, to the exact same seat and ordered an identical meal. We tried to make the thing happen again, but it couldn't for it only happened once. The beauty of something like the Greenbelt Festival is that it doesn't happen every weekend; none of us could stand it. Even if it did, pretty soon it would be the same old thing.

Right. Let's look for three things the Gospel says about how to be honest. First, we're all sinners — but we know that, so let me put it another way for when things are familiar we don't hear them any more — rather, every single one of us is flawed, we each have something wrong with us. I don't care who you are, or how perfect you are, something underneath the surface, something nobody knows about — or maybe something a lot of people do — we are flawed. Look at the disciples. They had all kinds of flaws — massive egos, fighting amongst themselves, really into power, constantly thinking they were big time hot stuff — and so do we.

The problem comes when, because we are Christians, we believe God forgives us and we become "born again" or "saved" or whatever term you want to use, and so now we believe we can't admit that we're still flawed. When I'm healed of my sin, when Christ comes into my life, I'm still flawed — though now I have the presence of the Holy Spirit, I have his forgiveness and love working in my life, but I'm still me. God didn't come into my life and then suddenly I'm organized and even-tempered. In other words, when Christ comes into your life, he comes *into your life*. He picks up and takes you, where you are. You are flawed – and you continue to be flawed – but the Good News of the Gospel is that *we all know that*, so who are we kidding? We all know we're flawed, I know you're flawed, you know I am, you know I've all kinds of problems in my life, I know you've all kinds of problems in your life and, most importantly of all, *we know God knows*.

I came across the following statement by A. W. Tozer: "To us who have fled for refuge to lay hold upon the hope that is set before us in the Gospel, how unutterably sweet is the knowledge that our heavenly father knows us completely. No tale-bearer can inform on us, no enemy can make an accusation stick, no forgotten skeleton can come tumbling out of some hidden closet to abash us and expose our past, no unsuspected weakness in our characters can come to light to turn God away from us, since he knew us utterly before we knew him and called us to himself in the full knowledge of everything that was against us." Now that is the Good News of the Gospel.

We don't have anything to be embarrassed or humiliated about! Remember when Jesus met the woman at the well? She was a prostitute, a woman of very low repute in a small town where everyone knew who she was and what she did for a living. Jesus asked her where her husband was, she replied she didn't have one, and he said, "You've had five and the man you're living with isn't your husband either". She was so blown away she ran through town shouting: "Come see a man who told me everything I've ever done!" Husbands are going to wives: "Honey, I'll take care of this. You just stay here."

What caused a woman with that kind of reputation, who knew everybody knew her, to run down the street shouting who she was? It was Christ, who had liberated her from her past. He had forgiven her and she was now able to stand up in front of everybody and say: "My past is real but it has been forgiven, and I can go on from here." We all should have no problem in admitting this, for it's the message of the Gospel – Jesus forgives us *just as we are*, loves us and takes us into his family.

We also need to recognize that there are very many lonely people, who feel isolated and alone and that no one understands or could possibly comprehend who they are. Do you now see why the Gospel is such Good News? In the midst of our loneliness comes the Gospel which says God understands and knows what we've been through, that he wants to come alongside and be right there with us.

A little boy once walked past a pet shop and saw some little black puppies inside. He fell in love with them and ran home, raided his piggy bank, asked his parents if he could have a puppy, they said yes, and he returned to the shop. He told the owner he'd like to buy a black puppy, and the owner said: "There're six of them. Choose the one you want." Five were together, but the sixth lay in the corner by itself. The boy chose that one, and the pet shop owner tried to dissuade him by telling him it had been born crippled

– "You won't be able to play with it or take it for walks. It'll just lie around. Choose another one." The boy then pulled up his trouser leg revealing a calliper and said: "I'll take that one."

Do you see why I'm a Christian? Because Jesus came to the pet shop and I was over in the corner, and he said: "I'll take that one." Jesus said: "I was on the cross, I know what suffering is and I know what Yaconelli's been through and what he's going to go through, I love him, I identify with him, he's not going to be alone, he's the one I choose."

Many of us think God doesn't *like* us – notice I don't mean *love*; there's a difference. Of course God loves us – he has to, he's God. He gets up in the morning and says: "I love you." Yeah, fine, we can handle that, it sounds very abstract, religious and interesting, that's terrific. But what *I* want to know is, does God *like* me? Does he like being around me? Some of us love our parents – but we don't like them.

Once I spoke in front of 200 high school kids at a camp. Afterwards a little girl called Dee Dee came up, looked at me for a while and finally she said: "Mr Yaconelli, can I talk to you for a minute?" I said sure and got into pastoral mode, thinking she was going to tell me some serious problem. She looked me squarely in the eye and said: "Mr Yaconelli, I just wanted to tell you that I like you."

I'll never forget her. You'll never know what that did for me; I ran outside yelling: "She likes me!!" Those words changed my life. I've always known God loves me, but I've wondered to myself whether God really *likes* me. Does he like my emotions and my ups and downs? Does he like my imperfections and my craziness? Does he like ME? I don't want to hear that he loves me, I want him to say that he likes me and enjoys being around me because I make him laugh.

Dan Taylor has written a wonderful book that brings together all the advice he gave his children when they were growing up. Called *Letters to My Children*, the following excerpt deals with the time his son told him a schoolfriend of his was weird – that he was a nerd who wanted to be his friend more than he did – and what should he do? Dan answers that question with this terrific letter:

When I was in the sixth grade I was an all-American. I was smart, athletic, witty, handsome – especially with my Vaselined hairwave sweeping back from my forehead. And I was incredibly nice. Things went downhill fast later, but for this one year I had everything. Unfortunately I also had Miss Owens for an assistant teacher. Miss Owens was a college girl who was practising on us. She helped Mr Jenkins, our teacher. Miss Owens also went to my church. She knew that even though I was smart and incredibly nice there was a thing or two I could still work on.

One of the things you were expected to do in grade school was to learn how to dance. My parents had some reservations about it, but since I was only twelve years old that was OK. Every time I went to work on our dancing we did this terrible thing – and I mean it was terrible. I hope this kind of thing isn't done any more. The boys would all line up at the door of our classroom, then, one at a time, each boy would pick a girl to be his partner. The girls all sat at their desks. As they were chosen they left their desks and joined the snot-nosed kid who honoured them with his favour.

Believe me, the boys didn't like doing this – at least I didn't, but think about being one of those girls. Think about waiting to get picked. Think about seeing who was going to get picked before you. Think about worrying that you'd get picked by someone you couldn't stand. Think about worrying that you weren't even going to get picked at all. And think about it if you were Mary. Mary's a girl who sat up near the front on the right-hand side. She wasn't pretty, she wasn't smart, she wasn't witty, she was nice – but that wasn't enough in those days – and she certainly wasn't athletic. In fact, she had polio or something when she was small. One of her arms was drawn up, she had a bad leg and, to finish it off, she was fat.

Here's where Miss Owens comes in. Miss Owens took me aside one day and said: "Dan, next time we have dancing I want you to choose Mary." She might as well have told me to fly to Mars. It was an idea that was so new and inconceivable I could hardly believe it. You mean pick somebody other than the best, the prettiest, the most popular? You mean pick somebody other than Linda, Shelley or even Doreen? And then Miss Owens did a rotten thing. She told me it was the Christian thing to do.

I knew immediately I was doomed. I was

doomed because I knew she was right. It was exactly the kind of thing Jesus would have done. In fact, I was surprised that I'd never seen a Sunday School flannel board that had ever said: "Jesus choosing the lame girl for the receiver dance." It was bound to be somewhere in the Bible. I agonized. Choosing Mary would go against all the coolness I had accumulated. It wasn't smart, it wasn't witty, maybe it was nice, but even I didn't want to be that nice.

The day came when we had to square dance, and I prayed secretly that God would work it out so that I would be last. Then, I could pick Mary because she'd be the only one left. No one would know, I would have honoured Miss Owens's request, I would have done the Christian thing to do and I would have got away with it.

You can guess where I was instead. For whatever reason, I was first in line. The faces of all the girls turned towards me, smiling. I looked at Mary and saw that she was only half-turned to the back of the room, her face staring down at her desk. Mr Jenkins said: "OK, Dan, choose your partner." I remember feeling very far away. I heard my voice say: "I choose Mary."

Never has virtue been rewarded so fast. I can still see her face undimmed in my memory. She lifted her head, and on her face reddened with pleasure and surprise and embarrassment all at once was the most genuine look of delight and even pride that I'd ever seen before or since. It was so pure that I had to look away because I knew I didn't deserve it. Mary came up and took my arm, just like we'd been instructed, and she walked beside me, bad leg and all, just like a princess.

Mary is my age now. I never saw her after that year. I don't know what her life's been like or what she's doing, but I'd like to think she has a fond memory of at least one day in sixth grade. I know I do.

The greatest day of my life was the day when the God of the universe spoke very loudly and clearly the words: "I choose Mike." That's the Gospel. He chooses us – flawed, sickly, messed up – and the God of the universe shouts out of the heavens: "I choose YOU."

8

Selling Out by Caving In

I have to say right off the bat that I'm not an intellectual or a sociologist. I'm trying to struggle with what it means to be a Christian in the nineties, in a world that is becoming more and more of something I don't understand.

I'm forty-nine years old, and am just blown away by the arcade video games kids play these days. When I ask them to explain what they're playing I get ten minutes of gibberish that only they understand – because this generation of kids thinks differently from the way I do.

They're able to think about three or four things simultaneously – listen to the radio, watch television, do homework – at least my kids have convinced me they can do that . . . This culture scares me because I'm worried that I'm losing touch and am unable to cope with it.

An American magazine recently asked: "Which would you prefer – (a) a wild, turbulent life filled with joy, sorrow, passion and adventure, intoxicating success or stunning setbacks; or (b) a happy, secure, predictable life surrounded by many friends and family without such wide swings of fortune and mood?"

I thought that was the stupidest question I'd ever seen; of course everybody chooses answer (a). That is, until I discovered many people chose (b) – they didn't want lives with super-highs and super-lows, but ones that simply ticked along. I hope, as you are reading this, that you've chosen (a) because if you've gone for (b) you've already succumbed to the paganism of this culture.

One thing that's different about the present than just five years ago is the stress we're all under. Have you noticed? Nine-year-old kids look like adults, for they're wearing £40 jeans. They can't play – what kid wearing £40 jeans can run and fall on the grass? Their parents would amputate their legs! Everybody nowadays dresses like an old person; nobody dresses like a kid any more so they can go out and have fun. I dress like an old person – *but I am old*!

We sense this stress, but what else is secularization doing to us? I don't believe secularization or paganism looks like secularization and paganism. When you live in Babel or Sodom and Gomorrah you don't know what sodomy look like because you've been so perverted by the culture you can't even define the sodomy that exists all around you. When we define paganism as debauchery, drunkenness and sexual immorality and limit it to that, we're in big trouble. Secularization is much more evil, much more subtle and sneaky in each of our lives than we ever imagined, and it has pervaded even the Church itself.

I feel this unreal pressure, and that's one of the thing that makes a secular society. We can't relax. We've all got to be doing something; we've got to have the music on or be off on some activity – just sitting there being absolutely quiet is maddening! That's terrible. Have you ever gone to church when silent prayer is asked for – even for a minute you can sense everyone muttering between clenched teeth: "Get it over with! I can't stand this. My stomach's going to growl before it's over." We panic because we can't handle silence. That's paganism and secularism – the inability to be quiet.

Rabbi Edward Cohn wrote a whimsical article about dealing with stress and said: "Life is tough. It takes up a lot of your time, all your weekends, and what do you get at the end of it? . . . I think the life cycle is all backward. You should die first, get it out of the way. Then you live twenty years in an old-age home. You get kicked out when you're too young. You get a gold watch, you go to work. You work forty years until you're young enough to enjoy your retirement. You go to college; you party until you're ready for high school; you go to grade school; you become a little kid; you play. You have no reponsibilities. You become a little baby; you go back into the womb; you spend your last months floating; and you finish up as a gleam in somebody's eye."

I want to know what happened to that gleam in our eye. And what happened to that gleam in somebody's eye before we were created? A. W. Tozer said: "Pagan society, secular society, takes the gleam out of its young people's eye." Paganism has taken from us all what I describe as "mischievousness", that little twinkle in our eye that says we're up to something. Wouldn't that be great if that was what was going on in all our eyes? Every time your pastor got up to speak in church he'd think: "They're planning something, I know it . . ."

That twinkle in the eye usually characterizes

couples who are in love. Have you noticed when it first happens they get this our-folks-think-we're-at-the-meeting-but-we're-sneaking-out look, that little gleam in their eyes? All of us ought to have that gleam in our eye. What is it that communicates to the world that we're Christians? That we walk around smiling, with "Jesus saves" on our T-shirt? That we don't smoke or drink? No. What really communicates to this world today is that we are people who are *alive* and *sneaky* and *mischievous*; we've got that little look in our eye that when we walk to the car everybody goes: "Uh oh, trouble is here."

You better believe it! We have the energy and life of the Holy Spirit who brings us alive and quickens us and enlivens us all to this world, and that's what communicates. Check out the books *Information Anxiety* and *Time Wars* – neither are available in the UK but I just wanted to recommend them to you – and here's a quote: "We have used our life, our literacy, our technology and our progress to create the thicket of unreality which stands between us and the facts of life. Experiences of our own contriving begin to hide reality from us, to confuse our sense of reality, taking us headlong from the world of heroes to the world of celebrities, transforming us from travellers to tourists."

Paganism, that is, a society that has become totally secular, takes its people and makes them tourists instead of travellers. It removes us from the actual act of living, so now we sit back and watch other people do the living for us. It has happened in the Church where we have speakers telling us how exciting the

Christian life is. We're not excited, but we love to come and hear people who are.

I now want to give three qualities of a pagan, secular society. The first is, *a barrage of information.* There're more and more books, magazines, publications, communications, computers – everything is just barraging us with more and more and more stuff. Even in the Christian world we've more books, more television, more magazines, more everything, overwhelming us. I don't know what to do any more. On my desk are a stack of books and another one of magazines – I just don't know where to start. I wish I didn't know how to read; I feel an incredible frustration.

The more a society becomes informed and worships information the less it seems to know. The more experts we have, with the more books, seminars and television shows, the more we begin to feel like we really *know.* The great thing about biblical truth is that in the Old Testament when they preached something and they talked about "knowing" it, it was like the sexual thing where it says "Adam *knew* his wife" – that didn't mean he just recognized her. That's what knowledge is really about; it's not just getting a barrage of facts, it's getting involved with those facts, letting those facts affect and transform my life so I don't just know *about* them, but that knowing them *changes the way I live.*

That's what the Bible is all about; I don't just read scripture, I don't just hear people talk about it, I don't just look at it, I don't just know it in my head – I know it to the point that it absolutely, totally begins to radically alter and change the way I live. That's knowing, and in this culture fewer and fewer of us know much of anything. We are barraged with information, we know all kind of facts, but we really don't know anything. The facts that we're learning mean nothing. It's like watching the weather on television – who cares?

The second thing is that *we have less discernment* because we have so much information coming to us that we're thinking less and are unable to recognize misinformation from disinformation from propaganda. We're not able to think carefully and to think carefully about the information we're getting. We're losing our critical ability to think.

In church we're not allowed to question the pastor. Wouldn't it be great if in the middle of our pastor's sermon we called out: "Excuse me! Hold it! What the heck are you talking about?" We all need to begin thinking much more critically. If someone were to ask me what it is that characterizes a Christian in the nineties, I'd say, first of all the look of mischief, and secondly, we're people who know how to think; we've maintained our brains and don't allow others to do our thinking for us.

The third thing about this scary information barrage is that we have more and more *a feeling of anxiety*. We feel there's something wrong, but we don't know quite what it is – nuclear war, economic disaster – something that tells us we're in trouble. We sense this and it's kind of scary.

I live in California and we have earthquakes out there. We take the ground for granted, but an earthquake totally freaks you out. Everything's shaking – the rooms, the houses – and it rattles you. From that moment on for the next few days, when you walk, you walk weird because you're afraid the ground's going to quake again. And that is the quality that describes this generation of people – we used to relax, trust and believe things were going to be OK, and I think there's a deep sense in all of us that it's *not* going to be OK, that something's wrong, and it's bothering and affecting the way we all live.

Another aspect of secularizm is *the emergence of the computer*. I don't think any of us realize its implications and what it is doing to us. But, first off, it's not evil – Satan doesn't live in a computer, although the Apple computer corporation's logo is an apple with a bite taken out of it . . . (only joking!). This computer generation has so changed our lives that none of us are aware of it.

It's ironic that in a culture so committed to saving time we feel increasingly deprived of the very thing we value. The modern world of streamlined transportation, instantaneous communication and time-saving technologies was supposed to free us from the dictates of the clock and provide us with increased leisure. Instead, there never seems to be enough time. What time we do have is chopped up into tiny segments, each filled in with prior commitments and plans. Our tomorrows are spoken for, booked up in advance. We rarely have a moment to spare. Tangential or discretionary time, once a mainstay and amenity of life, is now a luxury.

One of the clear results of this technological world – and especially of the computer – is that we now speak of nano-seconds. And because we speak of nano-seconds we're all being affected by this computer generation which puts this high premium on time. Why do we have all these time-saving devices yet we still don't have any time?

Here and now in the computer age time is controlling us; we serve it instead of it serving us. But Christians are people who are liberated from the slavery of time. We know how to be quiet – if Christ is really alive, he teaches us to be silent, how to be calm, to be patient. You want to read about love? Instead of 1 Corinthians 13 read the book of Hosea instead. In it God tells a prophet to marry a prostitute; sounds like a soap opera to me . . . The Old Testament is marvellous, telling through story, history and tradition what the Gospel is about. Read it.

In the computer age we *worship organization*, thereby becoming more organized but less spontaneous. The characteristic of Christian people we must maintain as long as we possibly can is our spontaneity. We're wild, crazy and unpredictable people – that's what communicates in a technological world, we're people where you never know what's going to happen, we have that look in our eye and it turns out it's really true. You never know what we're going to do or how God is going to work in our lives. That's why I love Jesus so much, because that's exactly the way he was. You think he was going to do this, he did that. His disciples would predict he'd do that, he didn't do it; that he'd say this, he didn't say it. Jesus was always doing what they didn't think he would do, and that, to me, is the great characteristic of Christian people, that you never can predict what we are – yet so many of us are so predictable.

Another aspect of this computer age is that we are *obsessed with speed*. We've got to go faster and faster and faster and faster. In a society that subtly worships time and speed, before you know it you're always in a rush, always walking just that little bit faster than normal.

And evil in society disappears – we no longer take it seriously. Evil is all around us; if we don't realize we're in a spiritual battle, that every decision we make is either moving us towards God or away from God, we're in trouble. Evil doesn't look like evil – it's not as depicted in the *Friday the 13th* and *A Nightmare on Elm Street* series of films; that's what it wants us to believe it is – but rather it's hurry, anxiety, pressure, stress. Evil always comes under the guise of something else, and its goal is the elimination of any thought of God or Satan.

The final characteristic of this pagan society is *the loss of the individual*. Don't you sometimes feel that you're nothing? You look at our culture and all the people on television and you think: "Gosh, there're so many people, there's so much going on, there're so many famous people I'm just *nothing*, a nobody." We become trivial.

In the States there's a newspaper called *USA Today*; God help Britain if it ever gets a newspaper like that. It's the best selling newspaper in America and was made for the nineties because it's full of little paragraph stories anybody can understand about celebrities. If you want to know what's happening with, say, Madonna and Michael Jackson, or Cher, it's in there. If you want to know what's happening with anybody who doesn't matter, read *USA Today*.

We are consumed and overwhelmed by trivia. I'm concerned that instead of talking about things that matter, Christians always end up talking about the things that don't. The description of a Christian in the nineties is that we know the difference, we know what matters. You think I'm kidding? OK. In the States we have a weekly magazine called *TV Guide* that tells you what's on in your particular area. Fifteen million peopl subscribe to it, and recently someone wrote to it asking this question: "Dear Sirs, If we have a nuclear war, will the electromagnetic waves caused by the dropping bombs damage my video tapes?"

Folks, we're in big trouble. This triviality — thinking about things that don't matter, focusing in on things that don't make any difference — is what characterizes pagan, secular people. Christians who love Jesus, in whom the Holy Spirit live, who are born again, are not necessarily people who don't smoke, don't drink, don't go to movies, don't do anything, but we *are* people who know how to think and not just to talk about trivia but deal with the things that really matter and make a difference.

In a secular society, where the individual doesn't matter, we're *afraid to take risks and make mistakes*. We're afraid to go out and do something new, different and scary. Secular society says not to take any risks, don't do anything that will embarrass or humiliate you, where you might actually have to suffer — just sit back, relax, and let us take care of you and serve you — that's "1984" and "Brave New World", but it's not the Christian world. The

Christian world says we take risks, we go out there and go for it.

With the loss of individual worth comes the feeling that *we no longer have any meaning*. Nothing we do matters. The world is telling us a lie: "You don't matter till you get old; till you have money; till you have power." That's not true! The Gospel says you have power, worth and meaning, *now*! I don't care how old or young you are, you can make a difference *right now*! You've got gifts the Church needs and needs to be using right now. You can minister to the elderly; tutor little kids; sit in the back and keep the minister honest – mid-sermon you can hold up cards with numbers one through ten on them – and on his toes.

In a pagan culture we are taught that we don't have any worth and value. Yes we do. But we feel we've lost our freedom, that we can't change or do anything. We can. And we're taught that whatever we do, whatever mistakes we make, whatever things we do in our own lives that are not what we want them to be, whatever we learned along the way where we blew it and got off track, there's nothing we can do about it, there's no hope. The meaning of the Gospel, above everything else, is that we are empowered with hope.

A black preacher friend of mine in Los Angeles called E. V. Hill once gave a talk about eschatology, the second coming, and the future, about the fact that we have hope as Christians, and the sermon was entitled "This ain't it!" You're depressed, you're down, life isn't looking too good; this ain't it! There's something else coming; this is not the end, there's a new age coming – God is not done yet.

That sense of hope and reality not only means that he is not done with the world, but he's not done with me. God can begin to take me and use me to accomplish great things for his Kingdom. We are not locked or impotent, we are not unable to change or to do what has to be done. We are not unable to change the world and, because of the reality of Christ, we can see our own lives change as well. That is the great news of the Gospel.

An evangelist friend of mind was preaching about how Jesus can change your life, and after the meeting there was a long line of people waiting to talk to him. A nineteen-year-old girl at the end of the line had to wait an hour before she could get to him. She explained to him that she was a drug addict and that when she was eleven years old her uncle began to sexually abuse her for two years. As a result of that, when he finally left her house she became so sexually loose she slept with every man she could and performed every vice imaginable. She lived under this shadow for years until that evening, when she said yes to Christ, but she was scared to death about what this would mean when she went home.

They prayed together, and later she wrote to him about what happened afterwards. She got back into her car with several other college girlfriends and began a late-night five-hour drive back. She fell asleep and had an incredible dream. "It was so real, it was like it was really happening, even though I knew it was a dream," she wrote.

"In my dream I was asleep in my bedroom and my uncle opened the door and walked in. He looked over at me, reached out his arms and said: 'Come to me.'

He was so compelling and I knew that if I got up from that bed and went to him, when I got back to school my conversion wouldn't mean anything. It was so irresistible and I didn't know what to do, when suddenly I heard a noise at the door. It creaked open, and there stood Jesus. He held his arms out and I ran past my uncle and threw my arms around Jesus. At that moment I woke up from the dream, crying, and all the other girls in the car said: 'What's the matter with you? What's going on?' and all I could do was cry out: 'I'm free! I'm free! I'm free!'"

Jesus stands with his arms outstretched, and as we embrace him he liberates us from the paganism of this culture.

9

The Fun of God

People think I'm very cynical. I'm not. But I think it's important to keep people a bit off-balance. So here for your delectation are some examples of different types of satire:

Healthy satire, or making people laugh at what they are uptight about. By making us laugh satire helps us admit our fears. It relaxes us and enables us to realize how we're not so weird and different after all. That's good, for it liberates us from believing that only we think a certain way.

In my satirical magazine called *The Door* we hold an annual award for the Theologian of the Year. Previous winners have included Woody Allen, Steve Martin and Tammy Faye Bakker. The following article was written before Tammy Faye's fall, and, as you read it, bear in mind that all the quotes it contains are genuine (it would be impossible to make them up!):

> "Being the wife of Jim Bakker, host of the world-famous 'PTL Club', hasn't been easy", so states the jacket of Tammy Faye Bakker's best-selling book *I gotta be Me*. The Keepers of the Door can only guess how difficult this must be for this year's Theologian of the Year who is also mother, television star, recording artist and noted author.

The choice of Tammy Faye Bakker as Theologian of the Year is a milestone in the history of our magazine because she is the first woman to receive this prestigious award. People ask us why. Well, to the many of us who have seen her on TV and who know all about her, there's only one way, and that's to read a selection from her book *I gotta be Me*. It's the story of Chi-Chi the dog.

"One day while eating dinner, little Chi-Chi, who liked lima beans, ate some and ran into the other room. I'd noticed that Chi-Chi had been losing weight and couldn't understand why. When the dog didn't return I wondered. Jim had seen the dog fall over on the carpet and not get up. I do that myself with lima beans. Jim went and checked Chi-Chi and then gently said: 'Tammy, Chi-Chi is dead.'

"I thought my world had come to an end. That was the first time death had ever entered into me. I'd never had anyone die that I'd loved so much. I wanted to run out into the street and scream. As I started to run out the house God stopped me in my tracks. I stood in the kitchen and couldn't move. I wasn't thinking about God, I was only thinking about why was Chi-Chi dead. God began to speak to me through an unknown tongue. I couldn't stop. It helped me keep me from falling apart. God is so good. He's there even when we aren't aware of him.

"At that very minute a real-estate agent wanted to show our house to somebody. Jim handed Chi-Chi to him and said: 'Would you dispose of Chi-Chi for us?' Jim put his arms around me and I cried and cried. I said: 'Jim, have them keep Chi-Chi for a couple of days. Please don't let them bury him right away because I know God can raise things from the dead.'

" 'Please don't let them bury Chi-Chi,' I prayed and I prayed. I expected Jim to bring Chi-Chi home at any minute. I knew God could do it, and Chi-Chi would be all right again. I expected to open the door and there would be Chi-Chi as usual.

"But the fact was that Chi-Chi was a naughty little dog. I loved him very much, but several times I'd wanted to give him away because he peed on our drapes, especially when he got mad at us. He'd chew on everything; we never knew what he'd tear up next.

"But you see, God knew how to take care of Chi-Chi for us. He knew if he took him that would be the end of wetting all over the room."

People ask if I'm being cruel by making fun of Tammy Faye Bakker. No, this was a chapter in a book that sold 60,000 copies. So this kind of satire isn't satire at all. What we did was simply reprint what she had written. We took it out of her book and put it all by itself and when people read it they said it was unfair. What do you mean? She wrote this! People were buying and reading it. And she didn't get one letter from anybody that said anything about that particular chapter.

On reading what Tammy Faye wrote we don't feel angry or upset because it certainly isn't a threat to modern Christianity. All we did was raise people's consciousness a little and show them what is going on all the time. We need to laugh at it. We need to look at this a little more strongly because this is not good theology. There's something wrong here and there's nothing wrong with pointing that out.

That's what satire does the best; it simply repeats what someone else has done and points it out. Because I'm an American I don't want anyone to feel left out, and *The Door*'s first international Loser of the Month came from England. Here it is:

Bertie the wonder dog raised over £500 for a village church – by peeing fifteen times in thirty minutes. Townsfolk in little Winterbourne, England, pledged to make donations to the church based on the number of times Mary Baylis' German shepherd lifted his leg during a thirty-minute walk. And the piddling pooch co-operated by wetting down every tree and post he passed.

"People might think it an odd way to raise money for the church, but being a farmer's wife I find it the most natural thing in the world", said Bertie's proud owner. "I made sure I had him full of liquids before we started out."

I simply point that out because I thought we'd seen everything there was to see about fund raising. Look. This really happened; nobody made this up. This is the kind of nonsense that goes on in the Church all the time, and if you happen to be a member of Bertie's church, what would you do? Would you just sit there or stand up and say: "Excuse me, but you've got to be kidding. You're not actually going to do this, are you?"

The Door also tries to come up with different ways to point out and ridicule the stuff that goes on. Once we did an issue on racism, a nice and honourable topic, so we decided to satirize the whole issue. We took our magazine and printed it to make it look like it had been photocopied. Then, we printed a red stamp on the cover which read: "We're very sorry, but we ran out of our regular issues. So we decided to send to you and people like you a copy."

People went mad! They wrote things like: "I've been a subscriber for fifteen years and I should have been one of the people who got a regular issue. I don't deserve a copy like this!" We had to explain to them that we were kidding and how it was a joke. There, satire was a little closer to home; people felt they had personally been discriminated against and they got angry about it even though we were doing an issue on racism.

People who get upset about racism often have the capacity for racism within themselves, even though they may talk and march against it. We can fall victim of the very same thing we join causes to protest against. Frankly, it's good to let people know that, otherwise if you happen to believe in something strongly you can get arrogant.

Arrogance, to me, is the biggest sin in the Church, and people exhibit it in so many ways – "You mean, you *haven't* spoken in tongues? You mean, you have not marched for the poor? You mean, you claim you're born again but you don't remember the exact date and minute?" – to intimidate the rest of us.

Those who know the Bible and can memorize every single verse make us, who don't know the Bible as well, feel like there's something wrong with us. Satire is a great way for people who think they've got all the answers to realize that maybe, just maybe, there's something wrong with *them*.

We've tried to point out other church issues. A church in the States once ran a tithing and steward-ship progamme where you signed a pledge card for "God's Ninety-day Guarantee Plan". On the first Sunday in January, when the four-thousand-strong congregation came to church, each person received a pledge card that read: "I promise to give ten per cent of my income to the church for the next ninety days." It then offered a money back guarantee if you weren't completely satisfied with the results.

I can't understand why the entire congregation didn't stand up as soon as the pastor announced this scheme and yell: "What? Are you *crazy*?" I don't ever remember Jesus saying: "Take up your cross and follow me, and if at the end of ninety days you're not completely satisfied I'll take it back."

So many churches think that doing something like this is "doing the Christian thing". They're doing the *opposite*! That's why I use satire – because it is a way of helping people see what they're really doing. And there's lots of other ways, for example, through a joke like this:

During the Second World War there were a group of men on a battleship sailing through the Mediter-ranean on a very foggy night. The man on watch was standing up on top looking out in front, hoping to see something. Suddenly he saw a light and immediately signalled down to deck using Morse code: "Send the following message. 'Alter your course ten degrees North.'" They sent the message and quickly recei   d the reply: "Alter your course ten degrees South." The watchman called for the captain, who came up and told him to send another message: "Alter your course ten degrees North. This is the captain speaking." The battleship received an instant response: "Alter your course ten degrees South. This is Second Class seaman Johnson speaking."

The captain was furious. He said: "Send the following message *right now*! 'Alter your course ten degrees North. This is a battleship.'" The immediate reply was: "Alter your course ten degrees South. This is a lighthouse!"

That joke speaks about a whole lot of things, about the arrogance and cockiness of people who think they know it all, about people who have a position and think it gives them the right to ride rough-shod over everyone else and simply to ignore reality. Frankly, in the Church and Christianity and in life, that kind of thing happens all the time. Satire calls people to those kind of issues.

We often get bored in church, and to help us through such life crises a book with the self-explanatory title *101 Things to do during a Dull Sermon* has been written to assist us. Here are a few suggestions:

★ Tuck a water pistol up your sleeve. See how many people you can baptize before they realize it's you.

★ Baptismal surprise: hide in the font or baptistry wearing a Creature from the Black Lagoon outfit.

Stay out of sight, but softly begin calling the pastor by name. When he finally stops his sermon and comes over to see who is calling, grab his tie and pull him in.

★ By unobtrusively drawing your arms up your sleeves turn your shirt or blouse inside out.

★ Try to raise one eyebrow.

★ Since it's obvious that your minister doesn't come from the same planet as you, decide where he came from – Mars, Venus, a black hole.

★ If you have a retractable ballpoint pen, take it apart and shoot the ink cartridge straight up into the air with the spring.

★ Make an empty chewing gum wrapper look as if there's still gum in it. Fool the person next to you.

★ Pretend to be four years old.

★ Try to indicate to the minister that his fly is undone.

Now, this book not only makes fun of churches and boring sermons, but also the real fun is that we've all thought of its suggestions. Where do you think they came from? Once I was in a church when a friend was preaching and I played the trick about the fly . . .

We shouldn't take life so seriously. Another great thing about satire is that *you never forget it*. It helps you to remember to keep your feet on the ground and stops you from worshipping yourself by thinking too much about who you are. Everything – including the things we love – should be up for satire – because we help improve them and make them better. Not all of us are satirists, but the more we don't take ourselves too seriously, the better off this world and the Church will be.

All satire does not have to be funny. Here's an excerpt from the book *All I really need to know I learned in Kindergarten*, published by Warner Press. It's not available in Britain – every book I recommend isn't available in Britain! The book satirizes our pre-Glasnost, pre-end of Cold War feelings about the Russians. It satirizes through pathos, through identifying deeply with the things that are really inside. It's a marvellous piece of satire, even though it doesn't appear to be:

> The Russians are a rotten lot; immoral, aggressive, ruthless, coarse and generally evil. They are responsible for most of the trouble in this world. They're not like us.
>
> That's pretty much the summary of the daily news about the Russians. But sometimes something slips through the net of prejudice, some small bit of a sign that it so clean and true and real that it wedges open our own attitudes.
>
> Nikolai Pestretsov. I don't know much about him, I don't know where he is now, but I'll tell you what I know. He was a sergeant-major in the Russian army, thirty-six years old, he was stationed in Angola a long way from his home, and his wife had come out to visit him.
>
> On 24th August South African military units entered Angola in an offensive against the black nationalist guerrillas taking sanctuary there. At the village of Ningiva they encountered a group

of Russian soldiers. Four were killed, and the rest of the Russians fled, except for Sergeant Major Pestretsov. He was captured, as we know because the South African military communiqué said: "Sergeant Major Nikolai Pestretsov refused to leave the body of his slain wife who was killed in an assault on the village."

It was as if the South Africans could not believe it. The communiqué repeated the information – "He went to the body of his wife and would not leave it, even though she was dead." How strange. Why didn't he run and save his hide? What made him go back? Is it possible that he loved her? Is it possible that he wanted to hold her in his arms one last time? Is it possible that he needed to cry and grieve? Is it possible that he felt the stupidity of war? Is it possible that he felt the injustice of fate? Is it possible that he thought of children born or unborn? Is it possible that he didn't care what became of him now?

It's possible. We don't know, or at least we don't know for certain, but we can guess his answer, his actions answer. And so he sits alone in a South African prison, not a Russian, or a Communist, or a soldier, or the enemy, or any other of those categories. Just a man who cared for just a woman for just a time more than anything else.

Here's to you, Nikolai Pestretsov, wherever you may go and be, for giving powerful meaning to the promises that are the same everywhere, dignifying the covenant that is the same in any language, which is: "For better, for worse, in good times and in bad, in sickness and in health, to love and honour and cherish unto death, so help me God." You kept the faith Nikolai, you kept it bright, kept it shining. Bless you.

Oh, the Russians are a rotten lot – immoral, aggressive, ruthless, coarse and generally evil. They are responsible for most of the troubles of this world. They are not like us. Sure they're not!

That's satire. And that's power. And beauty. It lets us know the wrongs that all of us commit in our arrogance and prejudice. Satire is a marvellous tool; it's very, very dangerous. We must be careful, but everybody needs somebody who loves us enough to satirize the things in us that are wrong.

10

Jerk-free Christianity

I'm not mechanically minded. Even if I follow the instructions to the letter, I still assemble things backwards. And in the book *All I really need to know I learned in Kindergarten* there's a story I really identify with. In this excerpt it's almost Christmas and the author's wife has told him she'd like one of those Bavarian cuckoo clocks with a nice little wooden house atop it. Now these clocks are really expensive, and one day he spies a cheaper one in a shop, but whose package carries the legend "Some assembly is required". Undaunted, he buys the cuckoo clock, takes it home and assembles it. Now read on:

> I put it all together with no parts left over thank you, and hung it on the wall, pulled down the weights, pushed the pendulum and stepped back. It ticked and tocked in a comforting kind of way. Never before had such an enterprise gone quite so well for me; the damn thing actually worked.
>
> The hour struck, the little door opened, the little bird did not come out, but from deep in its little hole came a raspy, muffled: "Cuckoo!" Three "Cuckoos"; that's all: The hands on the clock said noon. I peered deep into the innards of the Bavarian alpine goat-herd hut of simulated

wood. There was the bird. Using an ice-pick and a chopstick I tried to pry it loose.

I reset the clock to three. The clock ticked and tocked and then clanged. No bird. Out of the darkness at the back of the hut came a "Cuck . . ." but no ". . . oo". Applying the principle that I think we all know well, if it won't move, force it, I resorted to a rubber mallet and a coat hanger, followed by rigorous shaking. I reset the clock, the hour struck, the door opened. Silence. Close inspection revealed a small corpse with a spring around its neck. Not many people have murdered a cuckoo-clock bird, but I had done it. I could see it Christmas morning: "Here, honey, a cuckoo clock for you. The bird is dead." And so I did. I gave her the clock and I told her the story and she laughed. She kept the clock too, dead bird and all, for a while.

The clock and its bird are long gone from our house now and Christmas has come and gone many times as well, but the story gets told every year when we gather friends in December. They laugh, my wife looks at me and grins her grin and I grin back. She reminds me that the real cuckoo bird in the deal was not the critter inside the clock.

And me? Well, I still don't have a cuckoo clock of my own, but I kept something – it's the memory of the Christmas message on the package carton. It said: "Some assembly is required." To assemble the best that is within you and to give it away and to assemble with those you love to rekindle joy. "Cuckoo" to you old bird, and Merry Christmas to you, wherever you are.

I see the mechanics of being spiritual – of being a disciple of Christ – as being broadly similar. Just as not all of us know which end to hold a screwdriver, not all of us are spiritually inclined; indeed, most of us aren't quite sure what it means. Go to the Old Testament and check out Moses. He tended sheep for forty years until he day he came across a burning bush that wasn't burning up. God spoke to him from out of the bush, and, in introducing himself, described himself as the God of Abraham, Isaac and Jacob. That's the difference between Christianity and other religions – we serve a God who knows us personally by name. He then tells Moses he has seen the suffering of his people. If I had been Moses I'd have replied: "Well, why don't you come down and wipe out the Egyptians? Instead you sit around saying: 'I understand.' If you're really God, then why aren't you doing something about it?"

We still have that same problem – how come God isn't intervening in this world and taking care of it? Why isn't he fixing everything – my life included – around the world, and stopping the starvation and hunger in Bangladesh? But God says to Moses: "I've seen it long enough. Now I'm going to take care of it." I can see Moses then whooping: "All right!! We're wiping out those Egyptians! This is going to be great!!" Then God says: "Moses, I'm going to do it through you."

We live thinking about giving our lives to God. That's great until he says: "That means *you*." Then we shrug our shoulders and mumble: "Uh, I didn't really understand everything . . ." Like Moses, we all feel that sense of frustration, and, again like Moses,

when God points at us we stammer: "I can't do it!" If
you've been brought up on a non-stop diet of American
TV evangelists you'll expect God to declare: "Moses,
you can do it! Did you ever read the story of the little
train that could? I-think-I-can-I-think-I-can-I-think-I-
can. You just keep telling yourself: 'I can do it, I can do
it', and you will!"

Sorry. God said: "You're right, Moses, you are a
wimp!" Great news for those of us who want to be
disciples – God knows we're wimps! But he adds:
"Have courage, for I am with you. Moses, the issue isn't
you; the issue is me. Trust me. Put your weight on me.
Believe in me with all your heart and be committed to
me, because if you are I'll take care of it."

God, however, adds a little sting in the tail. He says:
"Moses, do you want to know how you can know that I
am with you and that you can trust me?" and Moses
nods his head. "After you get all the children of Israel
out of Egypt and away from slavery, you'll know."

Spirituality is not God telling us how he'll be with us
every step of the way, giving us the right signals so we'll
know to trust him. Rather, it's learning to trust him so
that after we've gone through dark days we'll look
back and go: "Oh, you were there. I see you now."
That's the issue when it comes to the Christian faith.

Here's a list of all the things you ought to have in your
life in order to be spiritual:

★ be a careful student of the scriptures.

★ be zealous and active in your stand for God.

★ have an appetite for worship and prayer.

★ be consistent in worship attendance.

★ practise scriptural memorization.

★ not be afraid of public prayer.

★ be active in the affairs of the local church.

★ fast regularly.

★ have a desire to stand against blasphemy and ungodliness.

★ have a firm grasp of basic, foundational theological truths.

Every time I've heard a talk or sermon on spirituality that's the list I get. It's a wonderful list, but there's a problem – this list characterizes the Pharisees.

Now, here's a list covering attributes of the disciples' lives:

★ poor knowledge of scripture.
★ concern about status.

★ lack of courage.

★ lack of commitment.

★ dishonest.

★ inconsistent.

★ having a temper.

★ failures.

★ confused.

★ poor theology.

★ prejudiced.

Other than that they were in great shape. The disciples didn't stay that way, but that's who they were. We hear so many talks on discipleship and being spiritual that are so heavenly minded they're no earthly good. They have us so far up in the clouds we don't know what it means for us to be disciples and actually have God use us.

Here are some pointers on what it means to be a disciple of Christ. Firstly, spirituality is *appropriate* – if you're four years old you act like a four-year-old; if you're ten you act like a ten-year-old. I used to think that if you were a disciple of Christ and "spiritual" it meant you acted like an adult. Discipleship is appropriate to where you are *right now*. That doesn't mean God doesn't call us to work on some of our rough edges, and it also doesn't mean we're called to become someone we're not. Our spirituality isn't tied to somehow changing and becoming *older*. The trouble is too many people act as though they're already dead. We need eleven- and fifteen-year-olds who love Christ and who express in their own way what the Gospel really means to them.

Spirituality is *practical*. Here are a couple of principles: *the significance of the insignificant*. Spirituality says that whatever I do as a Christian makes a difference, and that God somehow uses it to accomplish his will. Usually when we talk about spirituality it's as though only "spiritual" things really matter. They don't. Helping people with acts of kindness and thoughtfulness communicates the power of Jesus in your life.

Some of us think spirituality is a huge, gigantic, unbelievable deal instead of the little things that really *do* make a difference. For instance, a friend became a Christian after a guy who met him eighteen months earlier at a high school bumped into him again and remembered his name. He said: "I figured if you remembered my name there must be something to this Christianity stuff."

I can't remember everybody's name; I often can't remember where I am! You don't have to have my gifts or skills – and I don't have to have yours. The most seemingly unimportant thing can make all the difference in the world. A teeny weeny act of kindness can make all the difference. A fourteen-year-old high school kid concerned about homeless people in Philadelphia, Pa., went around his neighbourhood and collected some blankets, took them down to the inner city and gave them to the street people. The following week he did it again. Soon people heard about what he was doing and now there's an organization giving blankets to homeless people around the world.

That's all he did. He didn't print "Jesus" or the "Four spiritual laws" on the blankets, or tell the homeless people how to be a Christian; he just gave them blankets, a seemingly insignificant thing that made all the difference in the world to those people.

And that's what I love about Jesus. He was always doing seemingly insignificant things. When the woman caught in adultery was brought before him he started writing in the sand. Here's a humiliated, partially-clad woman at whom everybody is staring and yelling: "Prostitute! Whore!" Jesus is asked what the Law says should be done [kill her] and he writes in the sand. Without saying a word Jesus took the crowd's attention off the woman and onto himself. Tender, kind, gentle, silent, quiet, no big deal, he just got everybody to look at him instead of her.

That's what spirituality is – simple kindness, the

significance of the insignificant. When's the last time you wrote a little note to your parents telling them you think they're great? Really. That says more than all the religious and Bible talk, and will mean a great deal to them. It's an act of kindness any of us can do.

One day when I was a little kid in junior high school I got a new English teacher. She was the most beautiful woman I'd ever seen. That day she gave us a talk and told us: "Beauty is not what's on the outside; it's what's on the inside. Beauty is only skin deep. You have to get much deeper than that to find real beauty."

This made me feel guilty, so I decided to ask a girl I considered ugly to go to a movie. Our parents each drove us to the cinema, where we met. During the film I sat there thinking: "Come on inner beauty. Nothing's happening." Finally I couldn't take any more, so half-way through I got up, walked out and caught a bus home, leaving her in the cinema.

I totally misinterpreted what that teacher said. She wasn't saying: "Go out and marry someone you don't find attractive." She meant we should recognize that what's on the outside says nothing about what's inside, and the least you can do is show a little consideration to everyone. I didn't realize that. When you talk about the Gospel you don't have to become the sort of person whose head's in the clouds while running around, helping everybody, and solving all the world's problems. To live the Gospel means showing acts of kindness that communicate the reality of who Jesus is.

The governing principle in my life is that: "Something is better than nothing." This helps me get through the day because everything I've ever heard about the Christian life insisted that either you love God, or you don't; you either give a hundred per cent or zero per cent; you give everything or you give nothing. So it appears God has an all or nothing standard. Actually, that's an American value system and nothing at all to do with the Gospel. In fact, the Bible says God regards something as being better than nothing, and, indeed, that he loves to party!

Take the parable of the prodigal son. When he returned home after blowing all his money his father threw a party. Then there's the parable of the lost coin. When it was found, again a party. Even the parable of the lost sheep featured a party! That's what God does when we show up – he throws a party! He's having parties all the time!

God celebrates every move we make towards him; he doesn't yell at us about what we don't do. Like learning to walk; sure you wobble and fall – God sits back, loves us and watches us as we make mistakes, stumble and fall. But he picks us up again and keeps us moving. The trouble is, many of us give up and quit before we've given ourselves the chance to gain our balance and learn how to walk.

Another characteristic of spirituality in this day and age is *quiet* – we need to know how to take moments of silence. Make time and space to get away from noise and be by yourself so as to make sense out of your thoughts. As the American Christian author Eugene Peterson says: "We need the quality of disengagment" – that is, to learn how to disengage ourselves from the hectic activity of this culture and this society. You don't have to be a monk or go to a monastry; just be quiet for thirty minutes. That's all! Some of us are never absolutely silent until we go to sleep – but even then there's a personal stereo stuffed in our ears. Being quiet means we know how to listen. People today don't need yet another sermon but someone who cares enough about them to reach out, hold their hand and listen to them.

Do you know how I know I have worth? Because the God of the universe, who created this gigantic universe that's so huge and complex I can't even fathom or understand it, who is so big and eternal, listens to *me*! Whoa!! That's what worship is – I pray and perform before God because I know he listens to me. And how do Christians communicate their faith in the nineties? By shutting up long enough to listen to the longings, heartaches and loneliness of the world around us. That communicates spirituality, and we all can do that! You don't have to go to discipleship school or seminary, go to church every Sunday or know the Bible by heart, all you've got to do is keep your mouth shut long enough to listen to someone else for a change. God speaks more through our quiet and silence than he does through the noise of this culture.

The fourth characteristic of spirituality is *passion* – we, in response to God, are passionate about our faith. We weep about it, laugh about it, become emotional and intense about it, we get angry about it – when all those feelings go through our minds it's all part of our expression and response to who God is. Perhaps that's why Peter is such a popular disciple. He was a walking emotional disaster with unrestrained passion.

When it comes to communication there are three levels of language. Level two is the level of *information*, the language of education – learning to name things, facts and figures. Level three is the level of *motivation*, the language of advertising and politics – to manipulate and inspire people to action. And in the nineties these two levels are becoming more dominant in everyday life.

There's another level – level one, the level of *intimacy*, which you first learn as a baby when you begin to say: "Mama . . . papa . . . daddy . . . ga ga . . ." Sometimes our desire to communicate with God may be so earnest, intimate and passionate, we go beyond vocabulary and use words we don't understand – that's why some people speak in tongues; they don't know what else to do! It's trying to utter the unutterable. So many different emotions inside us cannot be described and contained by systematic theology, but may be embraced by intimate prayer at the level of "Abba! Father! Papa!"

God is not a monster, he's our daddy, our papa, our abba. We can pull his trouser leg any time we want to – he's our papa, that's all right, we don't have to wait until the service is over! Nor do we have to wait for "an appropriate moment". We can interrupt God any time we want because we have this passionate, intimate love affair with our father, our papa, our daddy – and that's what spirituality and discipleship is all about.

Another spiritual characteristic is that *we're growing*. We're constantly changing. Every saint I've ever read about didn't think he was a saint, though those who did weren't. A characteristic of sainthood is that the closer you get to God the further you feel from him, because you become more aware of sin in your life.

When we examine our lives we often get really discouraged. We think we don't measure up to God's expectations so therefore aren't very good Christians. Instead of being hard on yourself and beating yourself with the mental equivalent of a big stick, realize that this is evidence of how the Holy Spirit is working in your life. Millions of people attend church and talk about Christianity every Sunday, but never sense or feel anything's wrong in their lives. Christians, meanwhile, recognize they are growing, going through a period of transition and that God is working on their lives constantly. There's no room for arrogance and cockiness in the Christian life, if only because Christians admit how much work God has to do in their lives.

Finally, the Christian faith is lived *in community*. As individuals we need each other and we need the Church – as bad and screwed up and boring as it is. Even if you can't enjoy the service you can enjoy the relationships you make there, knowing that people love and care for you. We need that community for the Church really to function and to be the people of God.

The pianist Jan Paderewski once came over to perform a concert at a four thousand-seater hall in New York. It was sold out months in advance and one woman brought her nine-year-old son (who wasn't doing very well at his piano lessons) to hear a great pianist, hoping that would motivate him. Of course, he acted like any nine-year-old would, fidgeting and wriggling. Suddenly, just before the concert was due to start, he rushed on stage, opened the piano and, before a shocked audience, began playing "Chopsticks". Paderewski heard the commotion, walked over to the boy, got down on his knees, put his arms around him and whispered: "Keep on playing!" He then improvised an incredible concerto around "Chopsticks". As he did so he kept repeating: "Keep on playing! Don't stop, you're doing great. Keep going!"

That's how I view the Gospel. We walk on stage, start plunking "Chopsticks", God throws his loving arms around us and says: "Keep on playing! Keep on going!" Meanwhile he plays a beautiful concerto. Some day we'll all be in heaven together, and we'll get to hear that concerto God is playing in all our lives.

11

Virgins on the Ridiculous

The Kingdom of Heaven will be like ten virgins who took their lamps and went out to meet the bridegroom. Five of them were foolish and five were wise. The foolish ones took their lamps but did not take any oil with them. The wise, however, took oil in jars along with their lamps. The bridegroom was a long time in coming, and they all became drowsy and fell asleep.

At midnight the cry rang out: "Here's the bridegroom! Come out and meet him!"

Then all the virgins woke up and trimmed their lamps. The foolish ones said to the wise: "Give us some of your oil; our lamps are going out."

"No," they replied, "there may not be enough for both us and you. Instead, go to those who sell oil and buy some for yourselves."

But while they were on their way to buy the oil, the bridegroom arrived. The virgins who were ready went in with him to the wedding banquet. And the door was shut.

Later the others also came. "Sir! Sir!" they said. "Open the door for us!"

But he replied: "I tell you the truth, I don't know you."

Therefore keep watch, because you do not know the day or the hour (Matthew 25:1–13).

This is a very intriguing parable. Every time I've heard this passage preached about, the crux of the sermon has always been, "they became drowsy and fell asleep." I would then feel guilty for I'd be getting even more drowsy. The preacher would say their problem was they got lackadaisical and ended up asleep when they should have been awake; they let themselves get drowsy and lulled to sleep, so that when the bridegroom showed up they weren't ready.

I believe that's a misinterpretation. The first thing about this parable is that *drowsiness and sleep are normal*. That's good news. I am tired of a Christianity that doesn't take into account that we're human beings, that we are people who need sleep, who – after we've worked all day – get tired and drowsy. Often the reason we fall asleep in church is not because Satan is in our heart but because it's *boring*. Since they're not talking about anything that has anything to do with our lives, we go to sleep. Simple as that.

The Christian faith – being "born again", being "saved" – is for human beings, real people who get drowsy and go to sleep. The trouble with so much of what I hear about the Gospel is that people always act as though being ready, waiting for the King – the bridegroom – to come, is like having to stay up all the time, as if you can't ever sleep.

This passage isn't telling us to deny our humanity. It was fine for the virgins to sleep, as long as they were *ready*, which didn't mean denying who they are. When we begin to think about being ready for Christ's return it's not some kind of spiritual voodoo, but rather it has to do with real life and real people who go through the real motions of everyday living. When Jesus comes back there'll be a lot of us working, many of us making love and others going to the bathroom. Do these activities mean we're not ready? Surely it's: "I'll be right there"; we grab our bags and off we go.

The Good News of the Gospel is that it is for real people – us – who are in the midst of getting our lives ready. I have a hard time with spirituality that denies our humanity. For example, when you first get married if your wife asks you to dig a ten-foot ditch you say: "Sure, honey, no problem. Anything you say is wonderful with me." And if her feet stink – "It's OK, I love you, it doesn't matter. They don't smell to me." After you get married, they still smell. Whether or not you're Christians, whether you love each other or not, that's reality.

The Christian life is like being married for, say, three months. I come home, see my wife in the kitchen washing dishes, walk up behind her and whisper in her ear: "Honey, I love you." Nothing. She doesn't even turn around, as though she doesn't hear me. So I say it a bit louder. Still no response. Now I yell, and she turns to face me and asks: "Do you love me?" "YES!!" "Then why haven't you painted the living room like I asked you to do two months ago?"

Now, when I tell my wife I love her, painting the living room is not what I'm thinking of. I don't like to paint! I hate painting. I thought when I fell in love with my wife and got married that one day I would walk in the house, she'd say: "Honey, will you paint the living room?" and suddenly music would start to play, I'd pick up the roller and say: "Of course I will, darling."

Love – responding to Christ – is wanting to do what you don't want to do because you want to. Love is choosing to do what you don't feel like doing because you realize that's what you need to do. So I paint the living room even though I don't like painting it. Just because I love somebody doesn't mean I like to paint it any more, but I realize I need to do that because I love my wife.

Christianity is the same. There're lots of thing I do for God and Jesus that I don't feel like doing. It's not some sort of romantic feeling where I'm floating around going: "Whatever you want me to do God, I'll do." There are times when I grit my teeth and mutter: "Fine. I'll do it. I love you, so here, I'll take the stupid thing."

Did Christ tell this parable to the disciples because they weren't spiritually prepared? The answer, of course, is no. Are any of us ready – right this second – for Christ to return? Is your life on some kind of plateau where you've arrived spiritually and are now sitting back saying: "Any time, God, I'm ready." I am never ever at the point. The myth that being spiritually ready means we *feel* like we're ready, we've everything – wife, kids, job – taken care of, we've read the Bible and prayed already this morning, and are in total spiritual control – life is wonderful – so OK God, come!

None of us are at that point where we think we're ready. None of us are at the place where we actually feel like we're ready. That's not the issue; it's *not*, do you get yourself to the place where everything is in place and your life is totally under the Lordship of Christ? It simply means, I know he's coming, my bags are packed, I'm out there doing the best I can and when he shows up I may be a bit surprised but, just a minute, I'll get my bags and I'm ready to go. It's not some mystical, weird deal, but a very simple and practical way of living every day, realizing he's coming – maybe when I don't feel I'm ready – but that's OK, I'm prepared.

But the five foolish virgins were too familiar with their faith. They brought their lamps, but no oil. Why? Because they really didn't believe they'd need any and besides, they'd have plenty of time. In other words, they'd done this so many times and were so familiar with what went on it didn't have any impact on their lives or mean anything any more.

Many Christians know a lot about Christianity, but they've become so familiar with it that it no longer changes their lives. The foolish virgins were so familiar with what was going on that when the moment came they really didn't believe it; they said they did, and went through the motions, but it really didn't make any difference in their lives.

People used to come and speak at my church youth group and ask: "How many people have you witnessed to today?" I'd mutter to myself: "I was *going* to", and feel really bad, for I thought that was what being a Christian was all about – a calculated decision on my part. When I flew on a plane I'd pray: "Lord, help somebody to sit next to me who needs to be a Christian." So as I sat on the plane I looked at every person walking past me and I wondered: "Is it them?" By the time it had filled up, my next seat was still empty. Or the person sitting beside me immediately fell asleep. Or, even worse, the flight was over and I hadn't exchanged a word.

The Christian faith is not something we force and plan how to live "Christianly". Rather, I let Jesus into my life and let the cards fall where they may. I do what I do throughout the day and if Christ is in my life, if the Holy Spirit is there, I don't have any idea how God is using that or communciating that, but somehow he makes a difference. I need to quit *calculating* what it's like to be a Christian and just let the Christian life flow out of my life. That's what it means to know God.

A nine-year-old boy used to go every morning with his businessman dad to a New York subwa station, wave him off, then return home with his mother. One day, after having said goodbye to his dad as he walked towards his mother a businessman late for work ran down the platform the other way. He didn't see the boy, collided with him, and realized that if he stopped to help the boy he would miss a very important appointment. Unsure what to do, he finally put his briefcase down and helped the youngster to his feet. The nine-year-old then asked him: "Sir, are you Jesus?"

That's what it means to be a Christian. It wasn't calculated; the businessman just did it. He didn't think about it and ask: "What's the Christian thing to do? What would Jesus have me do right now?" He struggled with it, but finally realized that helping the boy was what he needed to do. It was a pure, clean, spontaneous response to the presence and reality of Christ in our lives.

In the parable the real issue is that the foolish

virgins fell asleep and, when they were called to come and meet the bridegroom, they grabbed their lamps, took off and couldn't wait to get over there to be with him, but, because they were in such a hurry, they forgot to get oil.

The big issue in Britain, America and the West today is not Satan living in an AC/DC album, not Heavy Metal or backward masking, it's that all of us are in a hurry. We've got to get everything done *right now*, to get everything solved, resolved, taken care of right this second; we're in such a hurry we can't take the time to do the things that need to be done.

It takes time to be the people of God. It take time while we wait on God to do his work in us. Each of us has to *wait* for the truth to take hold, but we're in such a hurry and try to get things done so quickly we just can't let God begin to work slowly and carefully in our lives. He's doing things – we just don't know it. Just as we don't realize we're growing up, so it is with Christ in your life – the changes he makes takes time. For most of us it takes a while for God to smooth off the rough edges and get us to where we need to be in one particular area – and then he has fourteen other areas to work on.

We never get to the point where we've everything all figured out. God takes time. He heals us slowly and we learn lessons over a period of time; the trouble is, America has exported the idea that everything can be fixed by a pill, a book and a formula. Life doesn't work that way. Real life takes time. We need to take the time it takes to do what we have to do.

And the beauty of the Gospel is that sometimes it takes a long time for us finally to be ready to hear what Jesus has been saying to us all along.

A priest I know once had a twenty-six-year-old man come to him who had been married six times. An alcoholic, in despair he asked him: "Is there something the Catholic Church can say and do to restore me into the Church?"

The priest thought about all the things the man could do – indulgences, penances – and about what the Bible had to say about repentance. He took one hard look at him and, he recalled: "Finally I got in touch with what it must be like to be broken six times in a marriage, to live in an alcoholic fog since the age of twelve, and it broke my heart." He wept, threw his arms around the man and said: "Welcome home." Now that twenty-six-year-old was ready to hear what Jesus had been saying all along. Until now he couldn't hear it; now he could, and he responded to the Gospel.

Isn't that what's great about God? He sticks with us all the way. I pray we all listen carefully to God's voice and let our lives wait out until we're ready to hear his message.

12

Gift rapping

When you go to a religious convention you feel you've to give "religious" responses to questions, to act "spiritual" and talk about subjects like "giftedness". I mean, why is it the Church makes us all talk differently when we talk about God and Jesus? We talk normally until we talk about religious things. Maybe that's what's meant by speaking in forked tongues.

It's easy to get intimidated. How many times have you listened to some rock group on the radio when nobody was home and next thing you knew, *you* were a rock star? You'd grabbed the lead guitar – all you had was a towel on, you'd just taken a shower – and you're walking around the house doing an Eddie Van Halen, all the while having forgotten that actually your parents are at home entertaining guests . . .

We all do that. We dream of being somebody famous, so we lip-sync. I can't even do that well for I forget both the tune and the words. And we all sometimes wonder: "What in the world can I do for the Kingdom of God? Am I somebody who goes to Christian conferences and churches, hearing other people talk about it, or do I have a legitimate role in the Kingdom of God? Is there some place where I fit?"

I think there're five things that intimidate us and keep us from using our gifts. The first is *spirituality*. When I see really religious people at a Christian conference I immediately feel as though I don't measure up. Somebody gets up to talk and drones: "I read my Bible every day." Inside I squirm: "I was going to read it . . ." Already I'm intimidated. Then people stand up to talk about prayer or God or religion. Meanwhile I feel totally lost.

When we talk about God, we'd better talk about him the way he is. He is unbelievably passionate! When God made the world he didn't go: "Oh." I think he was up in Heaven yelling: "I'm going to make a world!!" The angels say: "Great. What's that?" and he replies: "Watch this!!"

When God created me, when I was born into this world, even though there're millions of people on the planet, I think that whenever every single one of us was born God was there in the operating room. When I was born God went: "WHHOOOAAA!! Ugly!!" But I believe God is totally passionate about *me*. Everywhere he goes, when someone asks about us, he pulls out a giant wallet and looks through it to pull out our picture. Yet most of us think spirituality is something boring and overwhelming, when in fact it is *who we are*. Spirituality is a great gift we have all been given; it's to be in touch with the creator God who is that passionate God.

We're passionate. When we go to church that's how we ought to be. But if somebody who is passionate comes in we look at him as though he's weird. When he raises his hands we say: "It's just down the hall to the left."

The second intimidating thing is *appearance*. In the West how we look is a big deal. Each of us knows how we look and what's wrong with our appearance.

Isn't that awful? When I was a kid I never worried about how I looked; I didn't know what *cool* was. Nowadays everybody does, even six- or seven-year-olds.

We're all intimidated by our parents who tell us our nose is too big or too small, our ears are too big or too small, our head's too big or too small, our hips are too big or too small, our rear end's huge or not. *Rolling Stone* magazine once ran an ad for 501 jeans featuring a guy wearing no shirt and showing off an unbelievable body. Take my shirt off and you'd never see the jeans . . . so I saw this guy wearing his 501s, his rear end super-tight in those jeans, and I bought a couple of pairs.

Recently I spoke to some teenagers in my home town and half-way through the meeting a girl raised her hand – I'm in a serious part, talking about Jesus – and asked: "Mr Yaconelli. Turn around!" I said: "OK", not knowing what was going on, and I did. She yelled: "Look! He doesn't have a butt!!" She was right; I don't. We get to this age where it shrivels up or gets huge – that's it.

Usually when we talk about spirituality and gifts many of us don't feel we're gifted because – why? – we're overweight, maybe we're not very good looking, we're average, we don't dress cool, we don't have much money. Already we feel God has no place for us for we're different, we're poor, we don't have everything we're supposed to have. That's rubbish. How we appear on the outside makes no difference to who we are inside.

The third intimidating thing is that *we transfer greatness into looks*. If you see somebody who's good looking you think they're a great person when you don't even know them. But what do you think of when you think of the disciples? Peter equals Rambo, a huge unbelievable guy; Moses, Samson; we think of them all like that. How do we know what Moses looked like? Perhaps in Heaven I'll bump into a short, wimpy guy with a lisp who looks *nothing* like Charlton Heston.

We feel intimidated because we don't look how we're supposed to look. The Gospel liberates us from worrying about how we have to look. We don't care. If we're overweight, so what? We don't go around apologizing for it. If we're teaching Sunday school and are heavy, we tell the kids: "Shut up, or I'm sitting on you!"

Another intimidating thing is *success and power*. Ever noticed how much, when we're around successful or powerful people, we admire them? Christian rock singer Charlie Peacock said he was once at a hotel and the receptionist said: "Oh, you're Charlie Peacock. Gosh, I'm sorry, I didn't recognize you." He replied: "You're sorry you didn't recognize me? I'm sorry I didn't recognize *you*."

Why do we always apologize around famous people? They should be apologizing to us for not knowing who we are. We have as much significance and importance and value as they do. That's what the Gospel says. Each of us has power, giftedness, significance and meaning outside of whether we're successful or a failure, whether we have access to power or whether we don't.

The fourth thing that intimidates us is *intellect*. When I meet intelligent people they're always quoting others – "As Kirkegaard once said . . .", you mean Bob Kirkegaard who works in McDonalds? I'm always intimidated by incredibly intelligent people. Although St Paul was probably quite bright, the Kingdom of God is full of people who weren't very intelligent – especially the disciples. They had no idea what was happening and never could figure out who Jesus was. That means good news for us all. The Gospel says that whether or not you have a giant intellect there's significance, value and worth in who you are.

The final thing that overwhelms a lot of us is *failure*. We let failure keep us from following God and knowing who he is, and from recognizing how it's through failure that we learn about spirituality. Someone put it this way: "I can't learn to walk without falling." In other words, the way I get my balance and understand what balance is by being able to fall.

I remember the first day my children learned to walk; it was wonderful – they were sixteen – and it was great. The way you learn balance and understand what it is through failure. Many think Christianity is not for people who fail, that it's solely for the successful, who love God with all their heart, give him everything they have and are always winning. That's a lie. Christianity is for those who are not afraid to fail. We are the people who are risky, scary and willing enough to go out there and blow it. If you're going to fail, at least do a good job of it!

What runs through our societ and tells us this? The first thing is that *only the best matters*. If you're not the best, the first, number one, you only partially did it, if you weren't really a star, then you're nothing. It's either everything – or nothing. You either love God, or you don't; you either hate God or you love him, there's no in-between – you're one or the other. We all live in the muddled in-between, but we're taught that we have to be the best, to be number one. If we're going to understand giftedness in the Church, then we have to realize it's made up of people who are every kind of in-between. We're all struggling along at different levels to each other – and we don't compare ourselves to each other either – we look ahead to Jesus and we go from there.

Secondly, *many of us don't know what our gifts are.* Because the only gifts we ever talk about in the Church are *teaching, administration, pastoring, nursing, helping*; you say, great, that's five; but I'm history, I can't do any of those. What is it about the Gospel that is liberating? That everybody has gifts they never thought of, gifts that aren't even listed in scripture. Cleaning the bog isn't listed anywhere, but it is a gift.

We should be excited about what God has called us to do – whatever it is. And if you aren't sure what your gift is, maybe God hasn't shown you yet. I get mad when people ask me: "What is your spiritual gift?" at conferences. "Uh . . . I dunno." "Before you leave this weekend I want you to figure it out." "Great. I have the spiritual gift of being stupid; I don't know."

Sometimes we don't learn what our gifts are until we look back. For others, well, we've never thought about it or asked ourselves: "What is my spiritual gift? What is it that God likes about me? What are the things about me that makes me really great?" When's the last time anyone told you how great you are? When's the last time you walked in to your house and your parents said: "You are so unbelievably great!" That's not what you hear; usually it's "You are so unbelievably *late*! You are so unbelievably *sloppy*! You are so unbelievably *irresponsible*!" They tell you all kinds of negatives; never once do they say: "You are gorgeous! You are terrific! You are unbelievable!" If they did that you'd think they'd flipped out.

Many of us don't know what our gifts are because no one has told us how unique each of us is. God has created you with a super-special giftedness that only you have; nobody else does. Because of that God has a place for you. You may not know what it is yet, but you will, and I have a feeling that a lot of us don't even think God says that to us. We think God sits up there glaring: "Oh yeah, you're gifted all right – if you just quit swearing, if you get a new hairstyle, if you get some hair . . . yeah, you're great, you're gifted – if you really give your life to God and start reading your Bible, if you really start praying." Look, take it from me – you're gifted, full stop. OK?

The third point is that *some issues aren't a matter of giftedness but a matter of choice*. If you're waiting to help the poor until you see that you have the gift of helping the poor, forget it! All of us, no matter what gift we have, have a responsibility to help the poor and needy, to be radical in our own lives, to do the things that have to be done. For some of us it's easy, for others it's a gift, but for many it's very, very difficult.

Again, sometimes our gift is our *past*. Some people

come from very rough backgrounds, have covered a lot of ground, been around and already made some unbelievable mistakes. The Gospel says, first of all, that our past is forgiven, but then it says something even more amazing – once your past has been forgiven, even your past becomes a gift by which you now can become an even more effective minister of the Gospel.

Remember the prostitute who came to Jesus? She cried and washed his feet with her tears. Why? Because prostitutes are passionate. Her past history of being passionate overflowed into her new life; she didn't worry about what other people thought of her. Jesus was the only one who saw that, even then, her past had become a positive thing, not a negative one.

Another thing that's great about the prostitutes who all hung around Jesus is that they weren't dummies. They were cynical; they'd been used and treated by men as objects, and were not fooled by phonies, but they reponded to Jesus's love for them as individuals. Our past has scarred us – sometimes it really affects us – but it is also part of our giftedness that God can use to accomplish the Kingdom of God.

In 1 Corinthians 12 is a wonderful passage of scripture. It says (v.22): "On the contrary, those parts of the body that seem to be weaker are indispensable, and the parts we think are less honourable we treat with special honour. And the parts that are unpresentable are treated with special modesty, while our presentable parts need no special treatment. But God has provided the members of the body and has given greater honour to the parts that lacked it . . ."

The parts of the body that seem unimportant have the most importance, and the parts that seem most important are unimportant. Good news! You are important! You are the one with the gifts! You are the Church!

Let's look at some spiritual gifts like *the gift of plodding* – being able to see something through to its finish, the gift of muddling along and getting something done, even if it's not very exciting. That is such a necessary gift in the Kingdom of God.

The next gift is *the gift of doubting*. Many people doubt all the time and make everybody – parents, Sunday school teacher, minister – mad because every time they say something you reply: "Well, I don't know. How do I know that's true?" and you irritate them. When doubting Thomas finally saw Jesus after having said he wouldn't believe until he saw the nail prints in Jesus's hands, Jesus didn't show up and say: "Hi Thomas, it's me, the guy you said didn't come back from the dead. Now it's your turn! You're history!" Instead, Jesus took Thomas seriously; he came and saw him specially to let him know this. Having doubts is a gift! The Church needs people like you to raise those kinds of questions.

Another gift is *the gift of earthiness*. I pastor a church for people who don't like to go to church, and my wife once told me that she didn't want to be a pastor's wife, having to go to missionary meetings. I said: "Great! That's why I married you." So here we are, after church we'll be talking away and she goes: "Aw, **** !" She says she doesn't know what it means, but her husband says it all the time . . .

Don't you like meeting down-to-earth people?

Maybe their language is a little rough and their lives are a little rough-and-ready, but so what? That's a great gift. We must keep touch with earthiness; we can't ever sanitize the Church. We have to be able to help people who are earthy as part of the fellowship of Christ, as part of the Church in order for it to have validity, in order for us not to lose touch with reality.

The fourth gift is *the gift of sensitivity* – being sensitive to other people's feelings. If you're that kind of person you'll get your feelings hurt over anything. Someone looks at you strangely and you start crying because you think they don't like what you're wearing. You automatically think it's you, and automatically feel bad. You have this incredible gift of recognizing and seeing what's going on, even though you never say much. You know what's great about this sort of person? When someone is hurting you're the first person beside them. You don't say anything, you may not know how to say it because you're shy – you have *the gift of shyness* along with the gift of sensitivity – and that's exactly what we need. We don't need someone who walks over and says: "What's the matter? Depressed?" "Not now, for I'm punching your lights out."

I don't need some big know-it-all coming over and telling me what's wrong and what I need to do. What I need is somebody shy, sensitive, caring, tender, gentle, who comes to me and loves me and supports me. Some people have that reputation; when someone has a problem, who do they go to? You. They're the ones always calling you up. You don't have a girlfriend or boyfriend because you never can, for people have always got their problems and never ever treat you like a normal person – because you've got this incredible gift of sensitivity.

Men can have this gift too. It doesn't mean you're gay or feminine if you happen to be tender, gentle and kind. A lot of women like that; they don't like being with macho men. Gentle means you're not pushy, but kind, you take your time to get things done, without getting uptight.

Then there's *the gift of storytelling*. Some people are great storytellers and every time you're with them they tell great stories. A late friend of mine who was a school principal would sit with problem pupils and tell them a story. He had this brilliant ability to tell stories and weave them around to get people to respond as a result. Problem kids would forget they were in trouble and soon be back in school working again.

Another great gift is *the gift of depression*. Some of us are super-moody and act like we've had a lobotomy and can't ever laugh too much because we're a Christian, and can't ever cry too much because we're a Christian. All of us have a different emotional temperament. Some of us are happy all the time, some of us are sad most of the time. I bet most of us have in our bedroom, perhaps in a drawer, a bunch of poems we've written – you got mad, your boyfriend broke up with you, something went wrong, it was your period, you were super-depressed – when we were alone, and we wrote these poems we don't want anybody to know about.

But try and write when you're not depressed and . . . nothing happens. It was out of your depression and dark moments that this beautiful poetry was forged. That's a gift. I read somewhere that apparently forty-eight per cent of the great artists were manic depressives. Isn't that encouraging? That was part of their giftedness; they were super-high one minute, super-low the next and that's when the great art happened.

In the great book called *All I really need to know I learned in Kindergarten* there's a wonderful story. One night at the author's church he had to take charge of seventy kids aged four, five or six for an hour. So he decided to play the game "Giants, Wizards and Dwarfs". You get the kids to run around the room, then when they're all in this total frenzy and chaos you yell out at the top of your lungs: "Giants, wizards and dwarfs!" You decide what you are; if you're a giant you act like one and find another person and growl: "Grrr! I'm a giant!" At the same time they have to decide who they are — if they're a giant, it's a tie; if they're a wizard, they lose; and if they're a dwarf they win because they can sneak between your legs and bop you on the head.

So the kids are all running around like crazy and he yells: "Giants, wizards and dwarfs!" The kids all run around screaming what they are when suddenly he feels a tug at his trouser leg. He looks down at a little girl who says: "I was just wondering, where do the mermaids go?"

He replies: "Mermaids? There's no such thing as mermaids." She looks at him and says: "Oh yes there are. *I* am a mermaid." He answers: "Mermaids stand next to the Emperor of the sea", and he holds her hand. In the book he says not to tell him there aren't mermaids because he once held a mermaid's hand.

He asks: "Where do the mermaids go?" None of us are giants, wizards and dwarfs. We all ask: "God, where do I go?" and he looks at all of us and says: "You stand next to the Emperor of the sea. And don't tell me there aren't mermaids, because I've held their hand."

We're all mermaids. That's the gift God has given us.